ATTENTION, ~~ster Hospit~~
AND LEARNING
PROBLEMS IN CHILDREN

PROTOCOLS FOR DIAGNOSIS ~~WITHDRAWN~~
AND TREATMENT ~~FOR SALE~~

Warren A. Weinberg, MD
Professor of Neurology and Pediatrics
Departments of Neurology and Pediatrics
University of Texas Southwestern Medical Center at Dallas
Director of Pediatric Behavioral Neurology Program
Division of Pediatric Neurology
Children's Medical Center of Dallas
Dallas, Texas

Caryn R. Harper, MS
Faculty Associate
Department of Neurology
University of Texas Southwestern Medical Center at Dallas
Dallas, Texas

Roger A. Brumback, MD
Professor and Chairman
Department of Pathology
Creighton University School of Medicine
Saint Joseph Hospital

Please check
Disc/CD-RO
issuing

BC Decker Inc
Hami

BC Decker Inc
20 Hughson Street South
P.O. Box 620, L.C.D. 1
Hamilton, Ontario L8N 3K7
Tel: 905-522-7017; 1-800-568-7281
Fax: 905-522-7839; 1-888-311-4987
e-mail: info@bcdecker.com
website: www.bcdecker.com

01 02 03 04 / GAL / 9 8 7 6 5 4 3 2 1

ISBN 1-55009-161-1   Printed in the United States

Sales and Distribution

United States
BC Decker Inc
P.O. Box 785
Lewiston, NY 14092-0785
Tel: 905-522-7017; 1-800-568-7281
Fax: 905-522-7839; 1-888-311-4987
e-mail: info@bcdecker.com
website: www.bcdecker.com

Canada
BC Decker Inc
20 Hughson Street South
P.O. Box 620, L.C.D. 1
Hamilton, Ontario L8N 3K7
Tel: 905-522-7017; 1-800-568-7281
Fax: 905-522-7839; 1-888-311-4987
e-mail: info@bcdecker.com
website: www.bcdecker.com

Japan
Igaku-Shoin Ltd.
Foreign Publications Department
3-24-17 Hongo, Bunkyo-ku
Tokyo 113-8719, Japan
Tel: 81 3 3817 5680
Fax: 81 3 3815 6776
e-mail: fd@igaku-shoin.co.jp

U.K., Europe, Scandinavia, Middle East
Harcourt Publishers Limited
Customer Service Department
Foots Cray High Street
Sidcup, Kent   DA14 5HP, UK
Tel: 44 (0) 208 308 5760
Fax: 44 (0) 181 308 5702
e-mail: cservice@harcourt_brace.com

*Singapore, Malaysia, Thailand,
Philippines, Indonesia, Vietnam, Pacific
Rim, Korea*
Harcourt Asia Pte Limited
583 Orchard Road
#09/01, Forum
Singapore 238884
Tel: 65-737-3593
Fax: 65-753-2145

Australia, New Zealand
Harcourt Australia Pty Limited
Customer Service Department
STM Division
Locked Bag 16
St. Peters, New South Wales, 2044
Australia
Tel: 61 02 9517-8999
Fax: 61 02 9517-2249
e-mail: stmp@harcourt.com.au
website: www.harcourt.com.au

Foreign Rights
John Scott & Company
International Publishers' Agency
P.O. Box 878
Kimberton, PA 19442
Tel: 610-827-1640
Fax: 610-827-1671
e-mail: jsco@voicenet.com

CONTENTS

Production of this text was made possible

by a generous donation to

Creighton University School of Medicine

from

THE CIMARRON FOUNDATION

PREFACE

This handbook is written for the physicians caring for children and adolescents, as well as for parents and educators. The goal is to demonstrate to readers how easy it is to recognize and successfully manage the common learning disabilities and the two prominent behavioral causes of social and school failure (primary disorder of vigilance and affective illness). This small handbook is sized so that it can readily fit in the physician's coat pocket and will be accessible as a reference during the office evaluation of the child or adolescent who is not doing well at home or in school. Parents should use this handbook to ensure that their child's evaluation covers each area of potential learning deficit as well as the primary disorder of vigilance and affective illness (depression; manic-depressive disease: bipolar disorders). Once an appropriate diagnosis is established, the physician and parent can then team to follow the treatment protocols in order to develop a successful management approach. Educators can also use the information contained in this handbook to understand the child's diagnosis and their own role in order for the treatment approach to be successful.

This handbook emphasizes brain functions of language, both verbal and nonverbal, necessary for successful learning and communication rather than labels. Labels are offered in the various protocols and in Table 2 in Chapter 32.

Chapter 1 of this handbook explains the organized approach required of physicians, parents, and teachers in evaluating and managing children and adolescents with learning and/or behavioral problems. Chapter 2 details the historical information that needs to be obtained from an informed historian during the evaluation. Family history information is particularly important, since most learning and behavioral problems in children and adolescents have an underlying genetic basis. In this context, adoptive and other social agencies need to be aware of the information in this handbook in order to obtain the vital family history data from the biological parents (or relatives). Chapters 3 to 26 are individual protocols describing specific learning disabilities involving language/communication skills. Each chapter (protocol) is organized as follows: definition of the skill, normal development of the skill, assessment of the skill, behavior associated with deficits in the skill, and clinical picture of the child with such deficit. Using the same basic format, Chapter 27 details motor skills (praxias), Chapters 28 and 29 describe frontal lobe functions, Chapter 30 details logic, wit, and humor, and Chapter 31 discusses vigilance (a brain function necessary for attention).

Chapter 32 outlines diagnostic syndromes and common patterns of presentation of learning disabilities. Chapter 33 identify treatment/management options for the various learning disabilities involving deficits in communication/language skills.

Chapter 34 describes affect and mood (depression; manic-depressive disease: bipolar disorders) following the same structured format used for learning disabilities, whereas Chapter 35 is a treatment protocol for affective illness and Chapter 36 provides detailed medication tables.

The bibliography contains only 16 references, but each of these references includes extensive lists of citations that can be consulted.

This handbook is a culmination of over 40 years of experience and research in the field of learning disabilities, attention, and mood/affective disorders of children and adolescents. We want to thank the many thousands of young patients and their parents who contributed to our knowledge. In addition, we want to offer special acknowledgment to the philanthropists that made these years of learning possible: The Cimarron Foundation (Mr. and Mrs. Woody Hunt), the Caleb C. and Julia W. Dula Educational and Charitable Foundation (Mr. and Mrs. Orrin S. Wightman, III), Mr. and Mrs. Morton Meyerson, and the

Azoulay family (Mr. Abraham Azoulay). The University of Texas Southwestern Medical Center at Dallas and Children's Medical Center/Dallas deserve a special thanks for more than 25 years of support and confidence in our work.

We trust this handbook will help children and adolescents receive needed care. With a broader understanding of these problems by physicians, educators, and parents, with development of better medications, and with the increasing use of the latest technology in every classroom, we anticipate even more success for all children.

Warren A. Weinberg, MD
Caryn R. Harper, MS
Roger A. Brumback, MD

CHAPTER 1

APPROACHING THE PROBLEMS OF CHILDREN WITH ATTENTION, BEHAVIOR, OR LEARNING PROBLEMS

Learning and behavior problems affect approximately 30% of children and account for at least 5% of pediatric office visits. Attention-deficit hyperactivity disorder (ADHD) affects approximately 25% of school children, and these children are generally treated with stimulant medications. Thousands of children each year receive special programming for speech and language problems and for learning disabilities. In order to qualify for a college scholarship under National Collegiate Athletic Association (NCAA) guidelines (Proposition 48), athletes must score 820 on the Scholastic Aptitude Test (SAT) or 18 on the American College Test (ACT). In certain states, children must pass competency tests in order to progress in grade level or to graduate from high school; and student scores on standardized tests often affect a teacher's salary. Over the years, federal and state legislation has been enacted to ensure that children with a variety of learning and behavior problems can receive a free and appropriate education in the least restrictive environment (PL94-142, 1975: Individuals with Disabilities Education Act, 1990/1997).

Although physicians are often called on to provide diagnostic assessment, treatment, and advocacy for children having behavior or school problems, there have been few guidelines and criteria to help in this process. Even though the *Diagnostic and Statistical Manual of Mental Disorders*[1] (presently *DSM-IV*, 1994) provides diagnostic criteria, they are too complicated to be useful in the primary care medical setting. The *DSMs* also create a multiplicity of diagnostic entities, each with an individual set of symptoms that overlaps with other sets of symptoms, thus leading to each child having multiple "concurrent" diagnoses and comorbidity. This creates considerable confusion, indecision, and difficulties in providing pragmatic treatment.

This lack of readily applicable diagnostic protocols has caused many physicians to abrogate their responsibility for medical evaluation and treatment, instead relying on other disciplines to provide both diagnosis and management. Unfortunately, this lack of medical input means that outdated concepts, which do not take into account the modern understanding of the nervous system and brain-behavior relationships, are applied to the situations, usually with unsuccessful outcomes.

The assessment of the referred child with attention, behavior, or learning problems is no more complicated than the evaluation of the child presenting with a febrile illness. However, it requires that the physician employ a systematic approach to evaluating the child with attention, behavior, or learning problems. By using the protocols in this book, the complete office assessment of the child with attention, behavior, or learning problems takes less than 30 to 40 minutes and provides the physician with a firm diagnosis and treatment plan that will satisfy the family, help the child, and mollify the educational establishment.

Basically, the majority of the attention, behavior, or learning problems in children are the result of very few entities: (1) learning disabilities, (2) affective illness/manic-depressive disease (depression and bipolar disorders), and (3) primary disorder of vigilance. These entities can be readily diagnosed and managed by the protocols provided in this book.

Many medical and neurologic disorders are associated with learning, behavior, and attention problems. In some situations, the learning, behavior, and attention problems are secondary to the underlying disease process, for example, (1) progressive intellectual deterioration associated with brain destruction in adrenoleukodystrophy; (2) cognitive deficits due to structural brain abnormalities as occur in tuberous sclerosis; (3) fluctuating disturbances of cognition, mood, and attention in individuals with epilepsy; and (4) mood disturbances associated with metabolic disorders such as hyperthyroidism or treatment for another disease process (eg, mood disturbance associated with corticosteroid treatment in patients with asthma). However, many children with a medical or neurologic illness can have an additional primary learning disability, mood disorder, or disorder of vigilance.

Reference

1. Diagnostic and Statistical Manual of Mental Disorders. 4th ed. Washington, DC: American Psychiatric Association, 1994.

CHAPTER 2

HISTORICAL INFORMATION NECESSARY IN EVALUATING THE CHILD WITH ATTENTION, BEHAVIOR, OR LEARNING PROBLEMS

History should be obtained using a semi-structured, closed-ended interview technique:

- Ask very specific questions that have "yes"/"no," "too much"/"not too much," or "concern"/"not a concern" as possible answers.

- In addressing each bit of information to be obtained, the examiner must determine (1) if the symptom or behavior is present, (2) the quantitative level (frequency/duration/intensity), and (3) if it is a problem or concern to the individual.

- To determine the child's feelings, do not ask, "How are you feeling?" Instead ask, "Are you having any sad or unhappy feelings?" If the answer is "yes," then ask whether these sad feelings occur "a lot of the time," "some of the time," or "a little bit of the time." Are these sad feelings "too much?" or "not too much?" Are these feelings "bothering you" or "not bothering you?"

When obtaining history from family members, do not ask, "How was the pregnancy?" Instead ask, "Were there any difficulties during the pregnancy?" If the answer is "yes," ask, "What were the difficulties?" Common problems can be offered as choices, thus bypassing any difficulties that the family member may have in finding the right word (difficulties in naming or specific word recall).

The following information should be obtained:

- Developmental history
  - Prenatal difficulties
  - Perinatal concerns
  - Age of specific developmental milestones
    - Sitting (normal 6–7 months)
    - Walking (normal 11–14 months)
    - Speaking in short sentences (normal 20–30 months)
    - Toilet training (normal 2–4 years)
    - Riding a tricycle (normal 2.5–4 years)
    - Riding a bicycle (normal 5.5–7 years)
- Concerns of parents, school, or other family members regarding
  - Disturbance of feelings
  - Stability of moods
  - Sleep habits and sleep disturbances ("night owl" behavior; initial, interval, or terminal insomnia; primary or secondary enuresis; sleepwalking; night terrors; morning fatigue)
  - Eating behaviors (noting any dramatic change in food selection or weight)
  - Activity/energy level

- Compliance with rules or antisocial behaviors (fire setting, sex play, cruelty to animals, vandalism)
- Compassion, empathy, and ability to show affection
- Anxieties, fear, and phobias
- Obsessions and compulsions
- Social skills (the ability to relate and get along with others)
- Diligence
- Vigilance (tonic arousal, wakefulness): Does this child become "hyper" when sitting in school or in church, or become sleepy when reading or riding in a car? Is there loss of attention during tasks requiring that the child sit still?
- Learning disabilities: Difficulties with reading, spelling, writing, arithmetic (mathematics), listening, word finding, speaking, sequencing, or organization
- In sum, functioning (or adjustment) at home, play, and school
- History of any disease processes
  - Significant medical illnesses
  - Hospitalizations, surgeries, emergency room visits
  - Fractures
  - Seizures or epilepsy
  - Head injuries/concussions
  - Recurrent complaints (including headaches, stomach aches, muscle aches)
  - Allergies
  - Previous evaluations, diagnoses, treatments, and interventions (including educational, psychological, and neuropsychological test findings)

- Behavioral interventions and medication treatment (must include the results, both positive and negative, of any treatment, including medication response, the behaviors benefited, those that were worsened, and any side effects. These responses are important for both diagnosis and future management.)
- Family history (three generations: siblings and parents; aunts, uncles, and first cousins; grandparents; and great grandparents, great aunts, great uncles, and second cousins)
  - Neurologic disease (eg, epilepsy, migraine, presenile dementia, and degenerative diseases)
  - Birth defects
  - Mental retardation
  - Learning disabilities
  - Affective illness (depression, mania, and manic-depressive disease including a history of suicide and homicide)
  - Alcoholism and drug abuse
  - Tics, Tourette syndrome, obsessive-compulsive disorder
  - Hysteria (Briquet's syndrome or somatization disorder)
  - Sociopathy
  - Thought disorder (schizophrenia)
  - Sleep disorders (sleepwalking, night terrors, enuresis)
  - Narcolepsy (pathologic disorders of excessive sleep)
  - Primary disorder of vigilance (attention disorder, disorder of tonic arousal or wakefulness)

CHAPTER 3

RECEPTION OF SPOKEN WORDS

The reception of spoken words is the ability to receive (hear) spoken words (assuming normal hearing levels).

Normal Development of the Reception of Spoken Words

- Infants, toddlers, and preschool children look at a speaker's face and lips in order to understand spoken language (mouth movements and other facial gestures assist in understanding the words).
- Older children have less need to look at the speaker's face and lips to understand spoken language.

Assessing the Reception of Spoken Words

- Review the developmental history for ability to follow verbal instructions.
- Observe the child's ability to respond to spoken words.
  - Determine whether the child must watch your lips and face as you speak to the child ("lip reading").
  - Did the child often say "What?" or "Huh?" particularly if your face was turned away?

Behavior Associated With Deficits in Reception of Spoken Words

- Inappropriate responses to conversation if the child is unable to see the speaker's lips.
- The child makes noticeable attempts to view the speaker's face and lips.

Clinical Picture of the Child With Deficits in Reception of Spoken Words (Receptive Dysphasia)

In order to understand a speaker, the child will make noticeable attempts to be in a position to view the speaker's lips ("lip reader"). Although the child is seemingly interested in what is being said, if the child cannot see the speaker's lips, he or she will frequently not understand the conversation, will say "What?" or "Huh?," or will misinterpret the spoken words leading to inappropriate responses (eg, the child might answer the question "How old are you?" with a statement such as "I am fine").

CHAPTER 4

INNER SPEECH

Inner speech is the ability to recognize/understand spoken words.

Normal Development of Inner Speech

- Recognition of speech sounds begins in early infancy
- By late infancy, verbal commands elicit proper responses
- In toddler and preschool years, children understand and respond correctly to verbal directions and conversation
- Before adolescence, children recognize and understand *high-frequency words (ie, "grasp," "moist," and "coward")

---

*There are well over a million words in the English language, but only a few thousand are commonly used in everyday speech, and these are considered "high-frequency" words. Mid-frequency words are used in more formal conversations, and low-frequency words are used mainly in authoritative discourse (eg, a college literature course).

- During teenage years, mid-frequency words have meaning (ie, "freight," "drought," and "occupation")
- Adults increasingly recognize low-frequency words (ie, "serendipity," "foment," "litigious," and "impecunious")

Assessing Inner Speech

- Review the developmental history for evidence that the child understands verbal commands and conversation and uses age-appropriate words
- Observe the child in both verbal and nonverbal settings

Behavior Associated With Deficits in Inner Speech

- Poor eye contact
- Resistance in listening to words
- Avoidance of lip reading
- Preference for nonverbal activities

Clinical Picture of the Child With Deficits in Inner Speech (Auditory Verbal Agnosia)

The child will have difficulty understanding spoken words, will not lip read, and will be uncomfortable, irritable, and disruptive in verbal environments, whereas behavior in nonverbal environments is appropriate. The child prefers a pictorial or nonverbal environment and recognizes (understands) the meaning of "pictures" or images (visual objects, events, and happenings) but is unable to associate or store words to these images (impaired word-to-image representation). The child receives but does not understand spoken words.

CHAPTER 5

WORD STORAGE (INNER VOCABULARY)

Word storage encompasses the fund of words that are readily available for use and that drive the child into action. When words are stored "in sync" with their pictorial (visual) representations (image), the words have meaning, and then the individual can understand both the verbal and visual environments.

Normal Development of Word Storage

The storage (vocabulary), definition (word-to-word association), and use (word finding) of common nouns and action verbs are collectively referred to as *inner vocabulary* and begin soon after birth.

Assessing Word Storage

- Listen carefully to what the child says in spontaneous speech
- Ask the child to name various objects
- Ask the child to provide definitions of words
- Ask the child to provide a pictorial representation of the word

The ability to store and use age-appropriate words is assessed by having the child/adolescent define words and match them with their images (pictorial representations).

- Ages 6 to 8 years should be able to correctly define the words "baby," "name," "green," and "second"
- Ages 8 to 10 years should be able to correctly define the words "visit," "spring," "money," and "thought"
- Ages 10 to 12 years should be able to correctly define the words "grasp," "moist," "stride," "browse," and "coward"

- Ages 12 to 14 years should be able to correctly define the words "freight," "obsolete," "drought," "absorb," and "occupation"
- Ages 14 to 16 years should be able to correctly define the words "fortuitous," "vaguely," "judicious," "vocation," and "absurd" (mid-frequency words)
- Ages 16 years and older may be able to correctly define the words "serendipity," "foment," "impecunious," and "litigious" (low-frequency words)

If the child or adolescent is unable to verbally define age-appropriate words, offer three verbal multiple choices, one of which is correct. This bypasses difficulties with naming (specific word finding). If the child or adolescent is still unsuccessful, offer a pictorial representation of the meaning of the word and after a few minutes again ask the meaning of the word. Examples for children could be "house," "boat," or "road" and for older adolescents "foment," "impecunious," and "litigious" (Figures 1–3). If the child or adolescent is unsuccessful in verbally expressing the word meanings, present the pictorial representation along with three verbal multiple choices. Children and adolescents with poor word storage can improve their fund of stored words when presented with the verbal word and the pictorial representation (image) of the word at the same time. Storage of words "in sync" with their pictorial representations (images) is necessary for meaningful inner vocabulary to develop and for proper word usage.

Behavior Associated With Deficits in Word Storage (Word Storage Dysphasia)

- Difficulty with verbal communication, such as difficulty in responding to verbal requests and in expressing themselves verbally.

Figure 1. Pictorial representation of the word foment.

Figure 2. Pictorial representation of the word impecunious.

Figure 3. Pictorial representation of the word litigious.

- In contrast to those children with recall problems who can pick the correct word after prompting (ie, provision of a multiple-choice list), children with deficits in word storage cannot choose correct words when offered multiple choice.

- These children have a delay in verbal communication (developmental aphasia) and are verbally quiet, with limited speech; if this is an isolated developmental problem, these children are sociable with good nonverbal (gestural) communication.

- Speech improves with age, but they remain better "doers" than "talkers."

- Essays written when they become adolescents or adults consist mainly of high-frequency words.

- They often score poorly on standardized IQ tests since both verbal and performance sections require thinking with words or recalling words for responses, but despite low test scores, these children are normally intelligent.

- Their performance is often misinterpreted as indicating that they have "dull normal" intelligence or are "slow learners" because the low IQ scores match their poor performance in school tasks requiring the use of words either in naming or in thinking of the word to prompt activity.

Clinical Picture of the Child With Deficits in Word Storage (Word Storage Dysphasia)

The young child who has difficulty with word storage is verbally quiet but can have good primary social skills and can make friends easily in physical environments such as the playground or athletic field. The older child will still enjoy nonverbal environments such as video games. Because of their quiet nature, others can believe that children with deficits in word storage are "slow" even though they possess normal intelligence.

CHAPTER 6

SPECIFIC WORD FINDING

Specific word finding is the ability to recall common nouns and action verbs.

Normal Development of Specific Word Finding

Verbal communication begins in early infancy with cooing (phonemes), and by ages 20 to 30 months, children are communicating with words, often in sentences.

Assessing Specific Word Finding

- Listen carefully to spontaneous speech.
- Ask the child to describe the examination room, activities of the previous evening, or other easily recalled events; ask for the names of common objects, events, or specific activities.
- If the child cannot spontaneously answer using common nouns and action verbs, the examiner should give spoken multiple choice to determine whether the child has stored the words but is just having trouble retrieving them—thus, a word-finding problem. If the child is storing words but is unable to retrieve by naming, he or she will pick the correct response when offered multiple-choice options.

Behavior Associated With Deficits in Specific Word Finding

- Young children with defective ability to recall common nouns and action verbs are quiet ("good doers" but "poor talkers") and point rather than provide a word for a common object.
- Children (ages 5–7 years) do not enjoy the game "show and tell."

- Older children tend to use short (two- to three-word) sentences and struggle in naming objects.
- Adolescents avoid classes that require discussion or conversation.
- Adolescents and children with specific word finding difficulties prefer nonverbal pursuits.
- Adolescents and children with specific word finding difficulties perform best with multiple-choice testing format.
- In contrast to those individuals with defective inner vocabulary, who have difficulty storing words (see discussion of word storage in Chapter 5), individuals with defective recall of common nouns and action verbs are storing words but are unable to recall them spontaneously or by the process of naming.

Clinical Picture of the Child With Deficits in Specific Word Finding (Dysnomia)

This child frequently is called "quiet," "shy," and "reserved" and is a "poor talker" but is often a good listener and lip reader. The child may have difficulty describing what he or she sees, feels, or experiences and seems to search for words to say. Long pauses or sounds like "uh" and "err" will interrupt the child's speech while he or she searches for the word. Phrases like "what do you call it" or "you know" are also frequent. This child does not enjoy giving a speech or having to recite in front of a group (and may be terrified by the prospect). This child is a "good doer," skillful in nonverbal environments, and a good "worker bee" (but usually not a leader). Because the child cannot find the words to express his or her ideas and plans, he or she will often merely undertake the activity without telling others (which can be problematic). For example, the child might go next door to visit a friend without telling the parents or leave the classroom to go to the restroom or locker without asking permission from the teacher.

CHAPTER 7

NOMINAL RECALL

Nominal recall is the ability to recall proper nouns (nominals).

Normal Development of Nominal Recall

- Ages 2 to 5 years normally use proper nouns in spontaneous speech
- Ages 5.5 to 7 years should be able to state part of their birth date
- Ages 6 to 8 years should be able to recall single syllable names; this ability progresses with age to polysyllabic proper nouns (nominals)

Assessing Nominal Recall

- Ages 6 to 8 years: Tell the child that the examiner's writing pen was a gift from "Mr. Brill" or "Mr. Dietz." The child repeats that name five times and is then told that he or she will be asked the name after 5 to 10 minutes.
- Ages 8 to 10 years: Use a bisyllabic proper noun (eg, "Mr. Hertzberg" or "Mr. Rutman")
- Ages 10 to 12 years: Use a trisyllabic name (eg, "Mr. Ravenstein" or "Mr. Hertzenberg")
- Ages 12 years or older: Use a four-syllable name (eg, "Mr. Schwartzenheimer" or "Mr. Hertzenberger")

If the child is unable to recall the entire name, he or she should be given the name as part of a three-set multiple choice (eg, "Mr. Bill, Mr. Lott, or Mr. Dietz") from which to choose the correct response.

Behavior Associated with Deficits in Nominal Recall

The child who cannot spontaneously provide the correct name in age-appropriate nominal recall tasks but can choose the proper name from multiple-choice offerings has a deficit in nominal recall ability (the information was stored but could not be "recalled," "found," or "named"). For example:

- The preschool child with defective nominal recall, when asked "Where do you want to go?," may name a specific place but on arriving at that place may become angry because the place is not the same one that the child thought he or she mentioned.
- Older children have difficulty recalling the names of teachers, coaches, and sometimes even best friends.
- Problems with "fill-in-the-blank" tests that require recalling "names"; performance improves on "multiple-choice" tests.
- Language arts is an especially difficult school course because it requires the identification (naming) of the parts of speech (eg, identifying adverbs, adjectives, prepositions, etc).
- Social study courses (geography, history, art, etc) are difficult because they require the recall (naming) of proper nouns.

Clinical Picture of the Child With Deficits in Nominal Recall (Nominal Recall Dysphasia)

This child is unable to spontaneously provide the name of his or her teacher or coach or even some of his or her best friends (but can correctly identify them from a multiple-choice list) and can even say an incorrect name, embarrassing both the child and teacher, coach, or friend. For another example, when asked by a parent the name of the restaurant where he wants to eat, the child might say "McDonald's" and then become upset on arriving there because he really wanted to go to "Taco Bell," or when the parent asks the child whom she would like to invite to stay overnight and she replies "Sarah" but is upset when Sarah arrives because she really wanted Jane to stay overnight.

When asked questions that require the recall of proper nouns, the child may sputter and say, "you know . . . you know . . . what do you call it?. . ., who is it?," seeking assistance, struggling with nominal recall, or looking puzzled.

CHAPTER 8

WORD CONDUCTION

In order to speak, words must be delivered from the storage site in the brain to the area that will formulate the spoken word. This function is most easily demonstrated as the ability to repeat words that have been heard.

Normal Development of Word Conduction

The ability to repeat words begins at 12 to 18 months of age.

Assessing Word Conduction

- Observation of the child's speech and spoken interactions with family and friends
- Echolalia (spontaneous repetition of words) is normally evident during the toddler years
- Words are being spoken by ages 20 to 30 months
- Ages 6 to 8 years should be able to repeat individually the words "Methodist" and "Episcopal"
- Ages 8+ years should be able to repeat together the words "Methodist Episcopal"

Behavior Associated With Deficits in Word Conduction

- Spontaneous speech of younger children will often be seemingly unintelligible but can be understood by family members or peers.
- The child communicates well using speech (letter) boards or gestures.

- The young child with a word conduction deficit often stutters or stammers, but older children usually only stutter or stammer in particularly stressful situations.

- With increasing age, this child performs poorly when asked to repeat test phrases, but spontaneous speech becomes relatively clear.

▌ Clinical Picture of the Child With Deficits in Word Conduction (Word Conductive Dysphasia)

This child leaves out parts of words that are not purely phonemes or syllables. Young children with deficits in word conduction are very difficult to understand due to the incompleteness of the words and because the incomplete words run together. Interestingly, the child's peers or siblings can often understand what the child is saying, probably in part because of the child's good nonverbal communication and gestures (see also Chapter 19). Young children will resist repeating words, but as they get older, the ability to repeat words will improve remarkably.

The stuttering and stammering of some children can be explained by difficulty with word conduction. After struggling to express the word, the stutterer with word conduction problems will express incomplete words, whereas the stutterer with normal word conduction will produce a complete word. The stuttering and stammering associated with word conduction deficits have a better prognosis than stuttering and stammering from some other causes.

CHAPTER 9

WORD FORMULATION

Word formulation is the ability to produce spoken words (to speak).

Normal Development of Word Formulation

- Toddlers by age 18 months formulate and express single words
- Toddlers between ages 20 and 30 months can use words in statement form ("stringing words together" in speech)

Assessing Word Formulation

- Observation of the child's spontaneous speech and his or her ability to respond verbally to instructions
- Ages 6 to 8 years should be able to repeat individually the words "Methodist" and "Episcopal"
- Ages 8+ years should be able to repeat together the words "Methodist Episcopal"

Behavior Associated With Deficits in Word Formulation

- Impaired simple word repetition
- Difficulty formulating speech sounds and words
- Poverty of correctly formed spoken words but intact word finding, as evidenced by appropriate nonverbal motor response, such as making appropriate gestures rather than a word, using a speech board, or gesturing for someone else to answer (see also Chapter 19 about prosody and gestures)
- Lack of spontaneous speech evidenced by difficulty with describing the surroundings, objects in view, activities of the previous evening, or any other easily recalled events

▐ Clinical Picture of the Child With Deficits in Word Formulation (Broca-type Aphasia)

This child can understand words, as demonstrated by an ability to follow commands or respond appropriately to spoken directives; comprehension is demonstrated through actions. In a situation of sudden stress (particularly stress producing strong emotions such as pain, fear, or anger), the child spontaneously expresses words, particularly those that have been heard repeatedly. For example, the child who otherwise does not speak might say "ouch" when stuck with a pin; "no," "don't do that"; "leave me alone" when bothered; or "hi" or "I love you" in a family situation.

CHAPTER 10

STORAGE OF NUMBER GRAPHEMES

The written symbol for a number is a number grapheme, of which there are ten (0, 1, 2, 3, 4, 5, 6, 7, 8, 9) in the decimal numbering system. Storage of number graphemes is the memory for these written symbols.

▐ Normal Development of Storage of Number Graphemes

- Ages 2.5 to 3.5 years are able to match single-digit numbers
- Ages 3.5 to 5 years are storing single-digit numbers and can choose the correct single-digit number when offered spoken multiple choice (discrimination)
- Ages 4.5 to 6 years are normally able to name single-digit numbers
- Ages 6 to 7 years are able to name two-digit numbers

Assessing Storage of Number Graphemes

To evaluate the ability to store number graphemes, the examiner asks the child to name presented numbers.

- Ages 4.5 to 6 years should be able to name the numbers 1, 3, 6, 7, and 9
- Ages 6 to 7 years should be able to name the numbers 12, 20, 25, and 50

If the child is unable to name the numbers, the examiner should offer multiple-choice options (this tests retrieval by discrimination rather than by naming).

Behavior Associated With Deficits in Storage of Number Graphemes

- Young children who do not store number graphemes will be unable to choose the correct number even when offered verbal multiple choices but should be able to match numbers (unless mentally retarded).
- Older children and adolescents will have problems with arithmetic and higher math (preferring to use calculators and computers for numeric language tasks).

Clinical Picture of the Child With Deficits in Storage of Number Graphemes (Dyssymbolia for Numbers)

The young child initially experiences trouble counting and then has difficulty with adding and subtracting. The child prefers the use of a calculator. The child does not like games that use numbers like dominoes, dice, card games, or board games that require counting. Older children will have difficulty with arithmetic and mathematics in school. Adolescents and young adults will have difficulty with algebra and advanced mathematics. Some of these children will have associated clumsiness, be stimulus dependent, and have difficulty with planning and sequencing.

CHAPTER 11

RECALL OF PHONEMES FOR NUMBER GRAPHEMES (ARITHMETIC)

The written symbol for a number is a number grapheme, of which there are ten (0, 1, 2, 3, 4, 5, 6, 7, 8, 9) in the decimal numbering system. Arithmetic (defined as addition, subtraction, multiplication, and division) requires the recall of the proper phoneme for the number grapheme. Arithmetic also requires recall of additional graphemes, the arithmetic operators (addition, subtraction, multiplication, division, fractions, percentage, and decimal symbols, etc). *Written* arithmetic is the process of recalling (naming), sequencing, and spatially orienting numeric symbols on paper.

Arithmetic is the symbol language used for communication in mathematics but is not itself mathematics or logic (true mathematics). ("Arithmetic is to mathematics as spelling relates to history.")

Normal Development of Recall of Phonemes for Number Graphemes

- Ages 3 to 5 years count objects and people, add, and then subtract in spoken communication

- Ages 5 to 7 years perform one- and then two-digit written arithmetic problems

- Ages 7 to 9.5 years have a simple understanding of multiplication, division, and fractions but are usually unable to recall (name) the phonemes for the graphemes of these arithmetic operators

- Ages 10 to 12.5 years recall the phonemes for the graphemes of the arithmetic operators for multiplication, fractions, percentages, and decimals

Assessing Recall of Phonemes for Number Graphemes

- Ages 5 to 6 years should be able to correctly answer "How many pennies are in a nickel?"

- Ages 6 to 7.5 years should be able to correctly answer "What is $2 + 2$, $4 + 5$, and $9 + 11$?" and "What is $3 - 2$, $7 - 4$, and $13 - 6$?"

- Ages 7 to 8 years should be able to correctly answer "How many quarters are in two dollars?"

- Ages 8 to 9 years should be able to correctly answer "How many half-dollars are in five whole dollars?" and "If you had nine apples and three friends, how many apples could you give to each friend?"

- Ages 9 to 10.5 years should be able to correctly answer "If you had to walk 100 miles, and you could walk 10 miles an hour, how many hours would it take you to walk the 100 miles?" and "What is 4×2, 6×3, 8×9?"

- Ages 10 to 11.5 years should be able to correctly answer "What is 6×8, 18×3, 12×7?" and "If you had a pie and divided it into four pieces, what fraction does one piece of the pie equal?"

- Ages 10.5 to 12 years should be able to correctly answer "What is one-fourth as a percentage?"

- Ages 11.5 to 12.5 years should be able to correctly answer "What is 25% as a decimal?"

Behavior Associated With Deficits in Recall of Phonemes for Number Graphemes

- Failure on the age-appropriate numeric language tasks
- Preschool children have problems counting the number of objects or people in a room

- First- through third-grade children will try to use fingers for assistance in counting

- Fourth- through sixth-grade children will repeatedly fail to "memorize" multiplication tables

- Middle and junior high school students will fail to retrieve the phonemes for the arithmetic operators of fractions, percentages, and decimals

- Algebra, calculus, and differential equations appear to be "like a foreign language" for high school students

- Students prefer to use calculators to solve arithmetic problems

Clinical Picture of the Child With Deficits in Recall of Phonemes for Number Graphemes (Phonemic Recall Dyscalcula)

When the child is counting, he or she leaves out numbers in the sequence. However, in contrast to the child with problems in storage of number graphemes (see also Chapter 10 on storage of number graphemes), these children do enjoy board and number games and can discriminate numbers. Numbers have meaning to the child, but the child is unable to recall the correct phoneme for the number. Nonetheless, the child can make correct change and can use an abacus, counting blocks, or a calculator to solve arithmetic problems. They use fingers and toes to help them count. For algebra and higher mathematics, computers with appropriate programs are helpful.

CHAPTER 12

STORAGE OF LETTER GRAPHEMES

A letter grapheme is the written symbol for a letter (the alphabet). There are 52 (26 upper-case and 26 lower-case) letter graphemes in the English language. Storage of letter graphemes is the memory for these written symbols.

Normal Development of Storage of Letter Graphemes

- Ages 4 to 5.5 years normally have stored letters and can choose the correct letter when offered verbal choices (discrimination)
- Ages 5 to 6.5 years should normally be able to name letters

Assessing Storage of Letter Graphemes

To evaluate the ability to store letter graphemes, the examiner asks the child to name the written letter.

- Ages 4.5 to 5.5 years should be able to name the upper-case letters *A, B, C, D,* and *E*
- Ages 5 to 6.5 years should be able to name the lower-case letters *a, b, c, d, h, j, k, m, n, p, u, w, x, y,* and *z*

If the child is unable to name the letter, the examiner should ask him or her to identify letters using multiple-choice options.

Behavior Associated With Deficits in Storage of Letter Graphemes

- Problems with decoding written words (reading)
- Success in school occurs only in the situation of a "book-less curriculum"

- Older adolescents can become literate for reading (fifth- to sixth-grade reading level), but spelling, writing, and nominal recall (see also Chapter 7 on nominal recall) often continue to be severely impaired

Clinical Picture of the Child With Deficits in Storage of Letter Graphemes (Dyssymbolia for Letters)

The child having difficulty storing letter graphemes will not enjoy letter games. Reading, spelling, and writing will be problematic. Because of difficulties learning letters (and therefore difficulties reading), the child may repeat primary grades. The older child will manifest prominent reading, spelling, and writing problems.

CHAPTER 13

RECALL OF PHONEMES FOR LETTER GRAPHEMES (SPELLING)

Phonemes are the basic sound units of speech (eg, the "m" in the word "mat"). A grapheme is the written symbol for that phoneme. Spelling is the recall of the phoneme for the grapheme.

Normal Development of the Recall of Phonemes for Letter Graphemes (Spelling)

Spelling tasks are usually initially encountered during first grade (ages 6–7 years). Success in spelling requires a normal ability to recall the phonemes for letter graphemes.

▌ Assessing Recall of Phonemes for Letter Graphemes

Age-appropriate spelling tasks can be used to assess the ability to recall the phonemes for letter graphemes.

- Ages 6 to 7 years should be able to spell "it," "cat," "look," "stop," and "spot"
- Ages 7 to 7.5 years should be able to spell "hit," "hot," "hat," and "hut"
- Ages 7.5 to 8 years should be able to spell "work," "talk," "girl," and "went"
- Ages 8 to 9.5 years should be able to spell "should," "could," "phone," and "house"
- Ages 9 to 10.5 years should be able to spell "monkey," "elephant," "receive," and "friend"
- Ages 10 to 11.5 years should be able to spell "purchase," "ethics," "delicate," and "delicious"; the child is then considered literate for spelling

▌ Behavior Associated With Deficits in Recall of Phonemes for Letter Graphemes

- Failure on the age-appropriate spelling tasks when due to a deficit in the ability to recall phonemes for letter graphemes; errors consist of phonemic omissions and substitutions but with good phonemic misspelling (spelling words as they sound rather than as they appear in the orthography of writing; eg, "coud" for "could" or "shud" for "should" and "fone" for "phone")
- Younger children with this deficit often also have phonemic omissions in speech (eg, "pay" for "play" or "ello" for "yellow")

• Transpositions errors (eg, "friend" spelled "freind" and "receive" spelled "recieve") indicate an additional problem with sequencing (ordering) (see Chapters 16 and 17)

Clinical Picture of the Child With Deficits in Recall of Phonemes for Letter Graphemes (Phonemic Recall Dysphasia)

The child struggling with spelling will practice spelling daily, improving over the day after multiple repetitions, only to regress by the following morning. The child with the most severe problem omits phonemes (and thus graphemes) (eg, "shud" for "should"). A less severe deficit is characterized by a substitution (eg, "fone" for "phone"). Younger children make more omission errors, whereas older children make more substitution errors. Adolescents and young adults may be able to spell high-frequency words correctly but not mid- or low-frequency words.* Family conflicts often arise because parents cannot understand why, after repeated spelling practice, the child still fails the school spelling tests. The child's success in multiple-choice spelling tests demonstrates the normal storage of the correctly spelled words and an ability to discriminate but not recall these stored words (the deficit for most children is *recall* of phonemes for letter graphemes rather than *storage* of the phonemes and graphemes).

---

*There are well over a million words in the English language, but only a few thousand are commonly used in everyday speech, and these are considered "high-frequency" words. Mid-frequency words are used in more formal conversations, and low-frequency words are used mainly in authoritative discourse (eg, a college literature course).

CHAPTER 14

READING AND READING COMPREHENSION

Reading is the ability to decode (either visually or through tactile sense) printed words and say the printed word. Reading comprehension is the ability to understand (gain meaning and information) through reading. It can be demonstrated by explaining or putting into action what was previously read.

▌ Normal Development of Reading and Reading Comprehension

The development of verbal and written language communication progresses from matching to discrimination (choosing the correct response from multiple choice) and then to naming (word recall).

Normal development of reading and reading comprehension:

- Ages 3 to 5 years initially match, then choose from multiple choices, and finally name (recall) the primary symbols (colors, shapes, numbers, and letters)

- Reading (decoding/naming the written word) progresses from matching, to discrimination, to naming of letters (phonemic recall) and written words (reading)

- Reading begins after vertical and horizontal *input* strephosymbolia (reversals) disappears (eg, *naming* "*d*" as "*b*," "*t*" as "*j*," or "*6*" as "*9*")

- *Output* strephosymbolia (*printing* of "*b*" for "*d*," "*p*" for "*q*," "*j*" for "*t*") is not associated with deficits in the ability to decode words and actually indicates a favorable reading prognosis in young children with delayed reading. However, children with output strephosymbolia will subsequently prefer to write in a print style rather than in a cursive manner.

- Initially, reading is gestalt, that is, either knowing or not knowing the word presented

- Ages 5 to 7 years begins to name written words independent of print style

- Ages 6 to 8 years reads ("calls") high-frequency, monosyllabic words (eg, "dog," "cat," "work," "wish," "yard," "class")

- Ages 8 to 10 years reads compound words (polysyllabic words resulting from the combination of two monosyllabic words; eg, "baseball," "houseboat," "schoolhouse," and "football")

- Ages 9.5 to 11 years reads high-frequency, polysyllabic words (eg, "perhaps," "picnics," "delicious," "certain," "numerous")

- Ages 11 to 13 years reads mid-frequency, polysyllabic words (eg, "obsolete," "vocation," "occupation," "athletics," "facility")

- Literacy is the ability to read and understand high- and mid-frequency polysyllabic words (ages 10 to 13 years, fourth- through seventh-grade age)

Assessing Reading and Reading Comprehension

- Ages 6 to 7 years should be able to correctly verbally spell "dog" and label the word spelled backwards ("god"). This correlates with the ability to understand and read first-grade reading material.

- Ages 7 to 8 years should be able to correctly verbally spell "was" and label the word spelled backwards ("saw"). This correlates with the ability to understand and read second-grade reading material.

- Ages 8 to 9 years should be able to correctly verbally spell "tip" and label the word spelled backwards ("pit"). This correlates with the ability to understand and read third-grade reading material.

- Ages 9 to 10 years should be able to correctly verbally spell "not" and label the word spelled backwards ("ton"). This correlates with the ability to understand and read fourth-grade reading material.

- Ages 10 to 11.5 should be able to correctly verbally spell "live" and label the word spelled backwards ("evil") and to correctly spell "dial" and label the word spelled backwards ("laid"). This correlates with the ability to understand and read fifth- and sixth-grade reading material.

A child who can, *without* visual input, spell the words *not, live,* and *dial* backwards and correctly label them orally as *ton, evil,* and *laid* has achieved literacy and will report the ability to read and learn by reading. Formal testing of reading passages will also demonstrate reading and reading comprehension (Table 1). Reading comprehension must be tested using a multiple-choice format if the child/adolescent is unable to offer a correct response by naming.

Behavior Associated With Deficits in Reading and Reading Comprehension

- Children with deficits in reading are unable to read (name or "call") age-appropriate written words.

- Isolated deficits in reading do not occur, but deficits in reading occur in association with problematic spelling (errors in phonemic recall for graphemes) and nominal recall. If output strephosymbolia also occurs, then the graphic skill of writing will be defective (orthographic dysgraphia).

- The child or adolescent who is unable to answer questions after reading may not have a deficit in reading or reading comprehension but may have a deficit in the ability to recall and name specific words after reading. Such individuals are actually capable readers and even can enjoy reading but respond poorly to questions requiring the naming of what has been read. Normal reading comprehension can be demonstrated by examination techniques that require discrimination (multiple choice, true/false, yes/no, or putting information acquired from reading into action) rather than naming.

• "Poor reading comprehension" does not occur in normally intelligent individuals with the ability to read who read independently for either pleasure or information. Unfortunately, in schools, reading comprehension is usually examined by methods requiring naming (word recall), and children with difficulties in specific word recall after reading are often mislabeled as having poor reading comprehension.

Clinical Picture of the Child With Deficits in Reading and/or Reading Comprehension (Dyslexia)

The child with a deficit in reading ability is unable to pronounce (or act on) age-appropriate written words. The child struggling with the development of reading will often show discomfort, embarrassment, and sometimes tearfulness with reading activities. This child does not find pleasure in reading. Most of these children will eventually become literate and be able to read for specific information but rarely will reading be enjoyable. For example, they may read and follow directions in a cookbook, read the sports section of the newspaper for scores and statistics, read technical manuals (like auto repair or home repair manuals), or read comic books.

Interestingly, young children (ages 5.5–8 years) struggling with the development of reading who have output strephosymbolia have a good prognosis for the development of reading with increased age. But these children are left with a dysgraphia. Children with input strephosymbolia are more problematic and will not begin to develop reading until the input reversals disappear.

There is no such thing as an isolated deficit in reading comprehension (in other words, a deficit in reading comprehension does not occur alone). Most children who are labeled with a deficit in reading comprehension actually have a very specific dysnomia called "specific word finding dysphasia after reading." These children perform poorly when tested by "fill-in-the-blank" techniques (word recall) and actually have what is more properly termed "pseudo-reading comprehension dysphasia." Such children will perform well when examined by written or spoken multiple choice or when asked to put into action the information gleaned from reading.

Some children with disturbed vigilance will also have reading problems. Children with disturbed vigilance often become sleepy during reading ("I fall asleep when I read") and thus are inattentive to what they are reading (see Chapter 31).

Table 1. Sample Reading Passages

	Questions
Grade 1	
The boy has a ball. The ball is red. It is a small ball. The boy hit the ball with a bat. The ball went far.	What is the boy playing with? What color is the ball?
Grade 2	
Dan will walk to the store. Mother will give Dan some money. Dan plays with his new toy. Father does hard work on the farm. Father will eat a big meal.	What is the name of the boy in the story? What did Dan buy at the store? Where does Father work?
Grade 3	
Tom and Kathy walk to the red school-house. They both saw a movie in art class. Kathy is almost ready to go to the store. Tom asked Kathy to wait for him in front of the house. Tom laughs at the funny toys in the store. Tom likes to play baseball with his friends. Kathy likes to help her friends do their homework and play house.	What is the name of the boy in the story? What did the children see in art class? What sport does Tom like to play? What does Kathy like to do with her friends?
Grade 4	
Father builds automobiles at his business. His favorite automobile has a shallow red back seat and a deep front seat. Father paints the outside of the car white. Mother works at a toy store. She prepares special dolls that look like pioneers for the school program. She also builds wonderful doll cottages. The doll cottages have beautifully painted decorations. She gives the doll cottages to children who have no toys of their own. The entire family helps with this important work.	What type of business does Father do? What color did Father paint his car? What does Mother enjoy doing? To whom does Mother give the cottages?

Table 1.   Sample Reading Passages (Continued)

	Questions
Grade 5	
The class has started a unit on dinosaurs in their science class. They have visited the Natural History Museum and the city Science Museum in order to gather new information about various types of dinosaurs. The most interesting thing that the students encountered was the enormous Tyrannosaurus Rex at the Museum. The museum guide informed the class that this type of dinosaur was one of the most ferocious dinosaurs of the time. The students have enjoyed this particular subject at school.	What unit did the children study in science class? Where did the class go to gather further information about dinosaurs? Who taught the class about Tyrannosaurus Rex?
Grade 6	
Will and Peggy study science in school. They learn about the sun, the stars, and the planets. The teacher told them a funny story about a famous scholar who studied the equator of the earth. They were surprised to learn about the inventors who furthered human knowledge. Will attends a biology class and learns about many different animals. Will recognized a picture of the crocodiles and lizards that the teacher showed to the students. Peggy learns about healthy eating habits in her cooking class. The class is growing tomato plants for a school project. They hope to enter the project in the annual science fair.	What is the name of the girl in the story? What were the children studying in science class? What was the class hoping to do with the tomato plants they grew?
Grade 7	
Over the past summers, our family has taken numerous vacations to various parts of the United States. The most fascinating recent trip was to an Indian cliff dwelling in northwest Colorado. During the expedition to the dwellings, the children were able to ascend to	Where did the family go on their most recent trip? What type of people did they learn about on their trip? Why did the children find this trip especially enjoyable?

Table 1.   Sample Reading Passages (Continued)

	Questions
the crest of the mountain. The guide led them to isolated habitats and ancient Indian ruins. The ruins were a fascinating glimpse into the past lives of the native inhabitants of the area. They also were able to explore the surrounding environment and investigate the native vegetation and animals. The extended journey to this part of the nation proved to be both educational and entertaining.	

Grades 8/9

The family is planning a summer camping trip to a famous mining town. Father hopes to teach his children about healthy outdoor living by exploring nature. Since camping can be treacherous, Father is carefully supervising all of the preparations. Paul and Joan will each pack their own burlap knapsack with the necessary camp supplies. Mother constructed a specialized apparatus to hold their immense tent. It is absolutely essential for Joan to receive swimming instruction before the trip because they will also be exploring by canoe a hazardous river. Paul has persuaded his father to visit a cave that bears once used for hibernation. The entire family is very excited about their much-anticipated trip.	What does Father hope to teach his children on their camping trip? What will the children pack in their knapsacks? Why was it important that Joan take swimming lessons?

CHAPTER 15

ORTHOGRAPHY (GRAPHIC ASPECTS OF WRITING)

Orthography is the ability to write legibly.

Normal Development of Orthography

- Ages 4.5 to 6.5 years often will demonstrate reversals in the printing of numbers and letters (output strephosymbolia)
- By age 7 years, output strephosymbolia should disappear
- Graphic quality of written symbols and their placement on the page improve over the ensuing years

Assessing Orthography

- Ages 5 to 7 years should be able to print legibly the numbers from 1 to 10 and the lower-case letters of the alphabet. If the child is unwilling or unable to work spontaneously, he or she can print from dictation the numbers 3, 5, 6, 7, and 9 and the lower-case letters *b, d, p, w, z, m,* and *n.* Lower-case letters represent a more mature response than upper-case letters.

- Ages 7.5 years and older should be able to write a story telling "what [he or she] did last night." Writing a brief passage allows the clinician to note graphomotor skills, sequencing, word use, spelling, and clarity of thought and to study in detail syntax and semantics.

Behavior Associated With Deficits in Orthography

- Reversals (output strephosymbolia) for letters (and sometimes also numbers) persisting past age 8 years are associated with difficulties with the graphic aspects of writing

- Reading ability, which can initially be delayed, usually rapidly improves toward adolescence
- The graphomotor aspects of writing remain laborious
- Printing, rather than writing in cursive, is preferred
- Written output is often filled with errors in grammar and syntax
- Children older than age 9 years who continue to print rather than write in cursive style have orthographic dysgraphia and, typically, a history of prominent strephosymbolia
- Often occurs in association with other deficits such as problems with phonemic recall (as shown in Figure 4)
- Children and young adolescents who write in single-line format rather than offer a paragraph often have significant difficulties with either organization, vocabulary, word finding, or all of these functions

Clinical Picture of the Child With Deficits in Orthography (Orthographic Dysgraphia)

Older children, adolescents, and adults with orthographic dysgraphia will prefer to print instead of writing in cursive. These children have handwriting that is difficult to read, and many will prefer to use a computer or word processor to compensate for this problem.

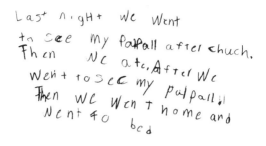

Last night We Went
to see my papall after chuch.
Then Ne ate, After We
Went to see my palpall,
Then We Wen t home and
Nent to bed

Figure 4. Orthographic dysgraphia and difficulties with spelling (phonemic recall) in a boy age 10.5 years.

CHAPTER 16

GLOBAL SEQUENCING

Global sequencing is the ability to sequence ("taking a whole, breaking it into parts, dealing with each part, and reassembling the whole; arranging the parts to complete a whole") and the ability to plan, organize, and perform in a sequence.

Normal Development of Global Sequencing

- Infants learn a sequence of the day's events (eg, the schedule for eating and sleeping)
- Toddlers are normally able to follow two- to three-step commands and can organize their play in sequence
- Young children ages 2 to 5 years are able to plan part of their day, anticipate and pursue activities in sequence, and follow multistep commands
- Children ages 6 to 11 years can anticipate and plan most of their activities, arrange toys, clean their rooms, follow an established routine for the day, sequence parts to achieve a whole, and break tasks into parts and re-sequence the parts to accomplish the whole
- Adolescents (and adults) plan and complete increasingly complex tasks and activities that require sequencing

Assessing Global Sequencing

- Normally, an infant should show alerting behavior in anticipation of feeding times and other daily routine activities
- Toddlers and preschool-age children anticipate daily routines, plan and carry out sequences, and demonstrate an organization to their play activity

- Ages 4 to 5 years should be able to count forward from 0 to 10
- Ages 5 to 6 years should be able to count backward from 10 to 0
- Ages 5.5 to 6.5 years should be able to say the alphabet
- Ages 6 to 7 years should be able to say the days of the week forward
- Ages 7 to 8 years should be able to say the days of the week backward
- Ages 8 to 9.5 years should be able to say the months of the year forward
- Ages 9.5 to 11 years should be able to say the months of the year backward

Behavior Associated With Deficits in Global Sequencing

- Difficulty playing independently
- Disorganized and has difficulty completing assignments in school and chores at home
- Requires frequent reminders
- Stimulus dependent (ie, doing what is suggested by the environment at the moment regardless of previous plans)
- Difficulty following a plan or carrying out a request
- Poor performance in response to open-ended commands such as "complete your work," "pick up your toys," "straighten your desk," or "clean up your room"
- Forgetting school homework
- Rushing through school assignments
- Careless errors
- Difficulty completing tasks
- Perform better in school in a "one-on-one situation"

- Difficulty in school with the sequencing of symbols, designs, objects, and events
- Transpose symbols in spelling and numeric language tasks ("girl" spelled "gril," "51" for "15")
- Difficulties with syntax (incorrect ordering of words or phrases)
- Right-left confusion

Clinical Picture of Child With Deficits in Global Sequencing

The child will be disorganized and will require frequent reminders to complete a task that when completed still has omissions (parents and teachers are particularly exasperated by the child's "forgetfulness"). These children will show difficulties in all tasks requiring sequencing including spelling, numeric language, syntax, and grammar in both speech and writing. Their schoolwork has numerous transpositions in spelling. The child wants to participate in activities but often does not sign up or show up to participate because of an inability to organize activities ("forgot" to come to baseball practice because doing something else: "Oops!"). The child is usually pleasant, kind, and truly interested in activities and in others but is easily distracted by any type of stimulus in the environment (to the detriment of any current tasks). Such a child will forget to sign up for the fall soccer program; forget or be late in inviting a friend for a "sleep over" and then wonder why the friend has not appeared by bedtime; complain about having nothing to do on a weekend because he or she did not arrange an available activity; or will be late for athletic practices and games, birthday parties, or other significant events. These children forget to do their homework or to hand in the completed homework assignment. They can be described as "a day late and a dollar short." The difficulties with event sequencing become significantly more problematic during episodes of depression.

CHAPTER 17

EVENTS SEQUENCING

Events sequencing is the ability to plan, arrange, and attend to daily activities.

Normal Development of Events Sequencing

- Toddlers normally assist in planning the activities of the day
- By age 6 years, children can independently anticipate, plan, and pursue activities

Assessing Events Sequencing

- Ages 4 to 5 years should be able to count forward from 0 to 10
- Ages 5.5 to 6.5 years should be able to say the alphabet
- Ages 5 to 6 years should be able to count backward from 10 to 0
- Ages 6 to 7 years should be able to say the days of the week forward
- Ages 7 to 8 years should be able to correctly state the days of the week backward
- Ages 8 to 9.5 years should be able to say the months of the year forward
- Ages 9.5 to 11 years should be able to correctly state the months of the year backward

Behaviors Associated With Deficits in Events Sequencing

- Difficulty planning and following through with planned activities, becoming readily distracted by environmental events, to which they respond immediately

- Are well meaning, with good diligence, intention, and volition, and may play appropriately but cannot avoid responding to momentary stimuli

Clinical Picture of the Child With Deficits in Events Sequencing

In contrast to the children with deficits in global sequencing, children with defective events sequencing have no difficulties with the sequencing of letters or numbers in spelling, numeric language tasks, or syntax/grammar in speech or writing. Otherwise, these children will have the same problems in life situations as do the children with deficits in global sequencing ("a day late and a dollar short").

CHAPTER 18

Symbol Sequencing and Symbol Orientation

Symbol sequencing and symbol orientation are the ability to maintain symbols in the correct order.

Normal Development of Symbol Sequencing and Symbol Orientation

- Children ages 3 to 5 years progressively match, then choose from multiple choices, and finally name from recall the primary symbols of colors, shapes, numbers, and letters
- Children ages 3 to 4 years are beginning to count
- By age 5 years, the child can use simple numeric language (eg, counting the number of people in a room)
- By ages 5 to 6 years, the child can correctly spell (both orally and in writing) his or her own name
- By ages 5.5 to 6.5 years, the child can recite and print the numbers from 1 to 10 in correct order and, subsequently, can recite and print (using lower-case letters) the alphabet
- Between ages 5 and 6 years, the child normally can differentiate right from left on others (ie, in extrapersonal space)
- From ages 6 to 8 years, children often lose the ability to differentiate right from left in extrapersonal space but gain the ability to differentiate right from left on themselves (ie, intrapersonal space)
- By ages 8 to 9 years, children develop full right-left orientation for both intrapersonal and extrapersonal space

Assessing Symbol Sequencing and Symbol Orientation

- Ages 4 to 5 years should be able to count forward from 0 to 10

- Ages 5 to 6 years should be able to count backward from 10 to 0
- Ages 5.5 to 6.5 years should be able to say the alphabet
- Ages 6 to 8 years should be able to answer correctly the question "What do 2 + 2 + 1 − 2 equal?"
- Ages 8 to 10 years should be able to answer correctly the question "What does 2 x 3 + 2 − 1 equal?"
- Ages 10 to 11.5 years should be able to answer correctly the question "What does 4 x 4 + 4 − 3 equal?"
- Ages 8 years and older should be able to draw a clock with placement of hands at 10 minutes before 2 o'clock. Observe graphic design, placement of hands, omissions of numbers, sequencing, placement of numbers, alignment, reversals, and rotations.

Behavior Associated With Deficits in Symbol Sequencing and Symbol Orientation

- Difficulty sequencing symbols in spelling and numeric language tasks (transpositions)
- Disordered writing (dysgraphia)
- Right-left confusion
- Associated problems in arithmetic sequencing (sequencing dyscalculia) are a result of errors in sequencing rather than of difficulties in the recall of numeric phonemes; for example, the child might correctly answer the problem 9×8 but would have difficulty solving the problem "$9 \times 8 + 2 - 1$" unless the task is broken into parts (eg, "What is 9×8, now $72 + 2$, and now $74 - 1$?")
- Transpositions rather than omissions of phonemes or graphemes characterize spelling errors; for example, "girl" might be spelled as "gril," "friend" as "freind," or "receive" as "recieve"

- Older children and adolescents are better able to read silently for comprehension rather than to read aloud (which requires sequencing, fluency, and enunciation)

- In graphic tasks such as the draw-a-person task, body parts are misplaced

- On the draw-a-clock task, the numbers and hands are improperly placed on the clock face (Figure 5). (Interestingly, numbers are rarely omitted, although younger children often place the numbers in a rotated or twisted position.)

- Writing has poor alignment and space use

- In severe cases, the writing runs off the right side of the paper and onto the desk

- The child will often draw lines on a blank sheet of paper to assist with maintaining proper alignment in writing

- Prefer printing rather than cursive writing (Figure 6)

- Artistic ability may be excellent

Clinical Picture of the Child With Deficits in Symbol Sequencing and Symbol Orientation (Developmental Gerstmann Syndrome)

The child with deficits in symbol sequencing will make transposition errors in spelling and have difficulties with syntax and grammar, in diagramming sentences, and in arithmetic and higher math due to the sequencing difficulties rather than retrieval problems. Difficulties with symbol orientation will account for defective handwriting, problems with alignment of symbols on paper, and errors in right/left orientation. These children will have difficulty with the handwriting course in school.

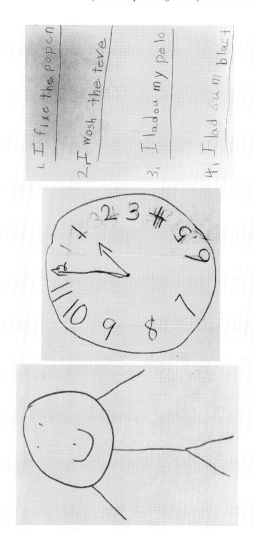

Figure 5. Phonemic recall (spelling) dysphasia in a girl age 7½ years, with developmental Gerstmann's syndrome.

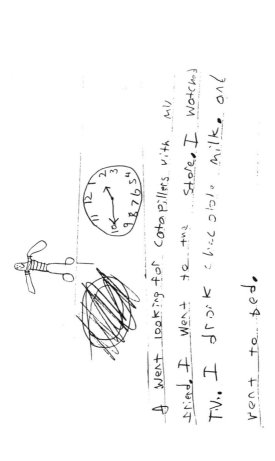

Figure 6. Developmental Gerstmann's syndrome with orthographic dysgraphia in a boy age 11½ years, who has no spelling problems. (Note the lines drawn by the child to assist with maintaining proper alignment.)

CHAPTER 19

DEFINITIONS OF PROSODY

The affective (emotional) interactive quality (tone) of gestures and speech (including pitch, intonation, and "ring" of speech) is fundamental for competent communication.

- *Receptive prosody* is the ability to understand the gestural and verbal prosody of others

- *Conductive prosody* is the ability to mimic gestural and verbal prosody

- *Expressive prosody* is the ability to look and sound appropriate relative to the feeling being conveyed and the social situation (how one wants to and should look and sound)

  - *Involuntary prosody* is the spontaneous affective and interactive quality of gestures and speech of the individual

  - *Voluntary prosody* is the volitional ability to express sounds or gestures with appropriate emotions

Normal Development of Prosody

Receptive, conductive, and expressive prosody are noted in early infancy as a primary form of communication (interaction).

Assessing Prosody

Involuntary Prosody

- To assess *involuntary receptive prosody*, the examiner observes the child's ability to respond appropriately to gestures and emotional elements of speech. To assess *involuntary expressive prosody*, the examiner observes the child's speech and gestures during play, during interactions with others, and in conversations. The child's speech and gestures are observed for blunted prosody or involuntary hypoemotionality (hypodysprosody) or excessive prosody or hyperemotionality (hyperdysprosody).

Voluntary Prosody

- To assess *voluntary reception of nonverbal (gestural) prosody*, the examiner asks the child to identify the appropriate face card (or the examiner's facial expression) of "happy," "sad," and "mad" (Figure 7)

- To assess *voluntary nonverbal (gestural) conduction of prosody*, the examiner asks the child to mimic the same face cards (or the examiner's facial expression)

- To assess *voluntary nonverbal (gestural) expression of prosody (recall and formulation of gestural prosody)*, the examiner asks the child to show facial expression for "happy," "sad," and "mad"

- To assess *voluntary verbal receptive prosody*, the examiner asks the child whether the examiner, when making a particular statement, sounds "happy," "sad," or "mad." For example, the examiner states, "I'm going to the movie tonight [or swimming, or to the store]," using the prosody/emotionality of "happy," "sad," or "mad" without the child being able to see the examiner's face.

- To assess *voluntary verbal conductive prosody* (repetition of verbal prosody), the examiner asks the child to repeat "I'm going to the movie tonight," telling the child to sound "just like I sound," using the prosody/emotionality of "happy," "sad," or "mad" without the child being able to see the examiner's face. Without looking at the child's face, the examiner notes whether the child is able to correctly mimic these emotions.

Figure 7. Example of face cards showing facial expression of happy, sad, and mad.

- To examine *voluntary verbal expressive prosody* (recall and formulation of verbal prosody), the examiner asks the child to express the proper prosody/emotionality of "happy," "sad," and "mad" using, again, the statement "I'm going to the movie tonight." Without looking at the child's face, the examiner notes whether the child expresses appropriate prosody/emotionality.

CHAPTER 20

RECEPTION OF NONVERBAL (GESTURAL) PROSODY AND UNDERSTANDING OF VISUAL IMAGES (PICTURES) OF EMOTION AND/OR OBJECTS

The ability to understand visual images (pictures) is required in order to understand gestures, body language, and nonverbal cues from others. Gestural prosody is one component of the visual environment that must be understood and stored as visual images (pictures) in proper relationship to words and other visual cues.

Normal Development of Reception of Nonverbal (Gestural) Prosody and Understanding of Visual Images (Pictures) of Emotion and/or Objects

- Infants from birth are visually alert, interested, and responsive to faces and other visually available objects
- Infants understand and respond to gestures of communication and visual images (pictures) in the world about them

Assessing Reception of Nonverbal (Gestural) Prosody and Understanding of Visual Images (Pictures) of Emotion and/or Object

To assess voluntary reception of nonverbal (gestural) prosody, the examiner asks the child to identify the appropriate face card (or the examiner's facial expression) of "happy," "sad," and "mad" (see Figure 7).

▋ Behavior Associated With Deficits in Reception of Nonverbal (Gestural) Prosody and Understanding of Visual Images (Pictures) of Emotion and/or Objects

- Children for whom visual images of emotion do not represent usable information have a deficit in nonverbal gestural reception

- Do not understand the visual-pictorial or the animated-gestural world about them and are "blind" to visual images of emotion (emotionally [affectively] blind)

- Avoid looking at faces; instead, they touch and explore faces, seemingly not visually recognizing the facial gesture, animation, or body language

- Do not respond appropriately to the gestures of others in communication

- Repeat words seemingly in an attempt to make sense of what they are seeing

- Words used in conveying emotion appear to be "out of sync" with the images associated with those words (thus displaying illogical behavior)

- Facial gestures suggest bewilderment in the visual environment

- Some children misunderstand and confuse common environmental objects and events, touch and inappropriately explore objects, and compulsively line up items

- Children not correctly storing images (pictures)-to-image (picture) and image (picture)-to-word representations display aberrant wit, humor, and logic

- There are some children who are only unable to recognize "mad" (or "sad" or "happy") but recognize the other two emotional gestures quite well. There are children who may be able to recognize objects quite well but not emotional gestures. Likewise, there are children who recognize emotional gestures but not objects.

Clinical Picture of the Child with Deficits in Nonverbal (Gestural) Reception and Understanding of Visual Images (Pictures) of Emotions and/or Objects (Receptive Visual Aprosodia; Visual Dyslogia; Pervasive Developmental Disorder)

These children are often labeled as having pervasive developmental disorder, looking and acting bewildered and confused about what is going on around them. They often touch, smell, and fondle objects in their environment that seem to have little meaning to them. They respond better to spoken directions than to gestures. Sounds have more meaning than the object itself. They may be fascinated by sounds and prefer objects that make noise, paying attention to the noise, not the object. They interact with people by touching. Older children continue to seem confused by happenings in the surroundings but often are verbal, with a large vocabulary and descriptive in what they say, but out of context with the activities about them. For example, they may talk in great detail about dinosaurs and outer space when supposedly participating in a game, helping in preparing dinner, or cleaning up an area. They seem to be "blind" to the visual environment and make little eye contact ("emotional blindness"), but they may respond appropriately to emotional sounds and words.

CHAPTER 21

RECEPTION OF VERBAL PROSODY

Reception of verbal prosody is the ability to understand the prosody of speech.

Normal Development of Reception of Verbal Prosody

- Infants respond to the prosody of familiar voices
- By toddler age, children are able to recognize the prosody of nonfamiliar voices

Assessing Reception of Verbal Prosody

The tasks used to assess receptive verbal prosody were noted earlier (Chapter 19).

Behavior Associated With Deficits in Reception of Verbal Prosody

- Understand the words and gestures but not the pitch, intonation, ring, and emotional quality of speech and thus are *emotionally (affectively) deaf*

Clinical Picture of the Child With Deficits in Reception of Verbal Prosody (Receptive Verbal Aprosodia)

This child does not respond to the emotional sounds of speech. The child cannot differentiate anger from happiness in a parent, sibling, or playmate and is unable to understand the warning in speech sounds. Severe punishment or abuse can follow a stern warning from a parent because the child does not understand the speech prosody and ignores the parent's warning. Meaningful communication requires that these children see the speaker's facial expression and other gestures because the prosody of the speaker's voice is meaningless. These children are not responsive to the affectionate tone of the mother's voice, but they are responsive to facial expressions and gestures.

CHAPTER 22

Conduction of Nonverbal (Gestural) Prosody

Conduction of nonverbal (gestural) prosody is the ability to mimic facial expressions and gestures.

Normal Development of Conduction of Nonverbal (Gestural) Prosody

- Babies are able to mimic (repeat) and communicate with gestures

Assessing Conduction of Nonverbal (Gestural) Prosody

The tasks used to assess conductive nonverbal (gestural) prosody were noted earlier (Chapters 19 and 20).

Behavior Associated With Deficits in Conduction of Nonverbal (Gestural) Prosody

- Gestures are constricted and blunted; facial gestures show little emotion and offer no assistance in affective interaction with others. However, deficits in conduction of nonverbal prosody are less problematic than deficits in the formulation of gestures (see below).

Clinical Picture of the Child With Deficits in Nonverbal (Gestural) Conduction of Prosody (Conductive Gestural Dysprosodia)

This child is often very expressive in speech prosody, but facial animation is stoic, with limited other gestural movements.

CHAPTER 23

CONDUCTION OF VERBAL PROSODY

Conduction of verbal prosody is the ability to mimic verbal emotions.

Normal Development of Conduction of Verbal Prosody

- Beginning in infancy, humans are able to mimic (repeat) verbal emotions

Assessing Conduction of Verbal Prosody

The tasks used to assess conductive verbal prosody were noted earlier (Chapter 19).

Behavior Associated With Deficits in Conduction of Verbal Prosody

- Verbal emotions are constricted and blunted. Difficulties with mimicking verbal prosody are less problematic in communication than difficulties with formulating verbal prosody.

Clinical Picture of the Child With Deficits in Conduction of Verbal Prosody (Conductive Verbal Dysprosodia)

This child's speech is monotone, but he or she offers appropriate facial animation and other gestures.

CHAPTER 24

FORMULATION OF NONVERBAL (GESTURAL) PROSODY

Formulation of gestural prosody is the ability to show appropriate gestures in communication.

Normal Development of Formulation of Nonverbal (Gestural) Prosody

- Begins at birth and is clearly established by toddler age

Assessing Formulation of Nonverbal (Gestural) Prosody

The tasks used to assess formulation of gestural prosody were described earlier (Chapters 19 and 20).

Behavior Associated With Deficits in Formulation of Nonverbal (Gestural) Prosody

- Gestures are constricted and blunted
- Animations show little emotion and offer no assistance in affective interaction with others
- These children understand speech and gestural prosody and mimic and express speech prosody
- Some individuals have excellent involuntary gestural prosody but defective voluntary gestural prosody; the opposite also occurs

Clinical Picture of the Child With Deficits in Formulation of Nonverbal (Gestural) Prosody (Ross-type Expressive Gestural Dysprosodia)

This child is unable to show in facial animation or other gestures the common emotions of sadness, happiness, or anger or complex emotions of being perplexed or frustrated. The child is able to show involuntary emotions, as expressed in laughter when tickled, crying when hurt, or a tantrum when angered. It is difficult for observers to read their facial expressions (correlate their facial expressions with their words or actions). There is an absence of animation and gestures in their communication. Verbal prosody is appropriate.

CHAPTER 25

FORMULATION OF VERBAL PROSODY

Formulation of verbal prosody is the ability to sound appropriately when speaking.

Normal Development in the Formulation of Verbal Prosody

- Evident at birth and is clearly developed by toddler age

Assessing Formulation of Verbal Prosody

The tasks used to assess expressive verbal prosody were noted earlier (Chapter 19).

Behavior Associated With Deficits in the Formulation of Verbal Prosody

- Speech is monotone and has a dull quality
- In communicating, children use gestures for meaningful expression
- Children with isolated difficulty formulating verbal prosody understand verbal and gestural prosody and conduct and express gestural prosody

Clinical Picture of the Child With Deficits in the Formulation of Verbal Prosody (Ross-type Expressive Verbal Dysprosodia)

This child speaks in a monotone voice, being unable to produce voluntarily emotional prosody in his or her speech. Gestural prosody is appropriate. This child must be understood in terms of his or her gestures and words rather than "how he (or she) sounds," which is monotone. In summary, this child is unable to express emotions in speech sounds.

CHAPTER 26

RETRIEVAL OF CORRECT VERBAL AND GESTURAL PROSODY

This chapter pertains to the ability to retrieve for expression the correct verbal and gestural prosody of emotions.

Normal Development of Retrieval of Correct Verbal and Gestural Prosody

- Begins in infancy with crying, cooing, and speech sounds of emotions
- By age 2 years, retrieval of correct verbal and gestural prosody is clearly developed

Assessing Retrieval of Correct Verbal and Gestural Prosody

The tasks used to assess expressive prosody were noted earlier (Chapters 19 and 20).

Behavior Associated With Deficits in Retrieval of Correct Verbal and Gestural Prosody

*Hyper*expression of prosody (*hyper*dysprosody/*hyper*emotionality)

- Characteristically have poor social skills
- Respond in ways that are seemingly "out of context" for the social situation by exhibiting overexpressive verbalizations, gestures, and actions

- Other people feel uncomfortable interacting with these individuals and often reject them

- When a little sad, may show profound weeping

- Minimal anger may produce immediate hostile, threatening actions

- A slight feeling of joy may result in explosive laughter

- Low-frequency or highly charged words are used in speech when high-frequency or less charged words would be more appropriate (eg, "scrumptious" rather than "tasty," "I would kill for that" rather than "I would like that")

*Hypo*expression of prosody (*hypo*dysprosody/*hypo*emotionality)

- These individuals appear expressionless, stoic, detached, or unruffled since they do not produce the expected facial or gestural animation in conversation

- Because they often feel uncomfortable in social situations, they are hyposocial, reject others, and are often "homebodies" or reclusive

- Difficulty communicating their feelings to others

- They epitomize the comment "you can't judge a book by its cover"; they are underexpressive in emotions

---

Clinical Picture of the Child With Deficits in Retrieval of Correct Verbal and Gestural Prosody

Hyperexpressive (Asperger's Syndrome)

The young child who is hyperexpressive from birth seems emotionally labile (dysemotional), demonstrating extreme, frequent moments of emotions with little provocation and requiring little stimuli to show such strong emotion. Examples include the physician's request, "May I listen to your heart?," which results in the young child responding with a loud scream, withdrawing, and striking out to prevent the examiner from getting close; the mother may ask for a hug only to find herself being strangled. The hyperexpressive child uses strong, exaggerated gestures and highly charged and often low-frequency words (rather than "good" they may say "scrumptious"). Other people reject the child because of his or her unpredictable responses in communication. These children do not appreciate other people's space (intrusive). For example, they may borrow others things without asking, join others at a table without being invited, stand nose to nose when conversing, be bossy and pushy, and sound excessively upset, demeaning, or belligerent, out of proportion to both the person's feelings and the situation, with a "hair-trigger temper." In some categorizations, these children are labeled as having Asperger's syndrome. Many of these children have a family history of affective illness and will themselves have symptoms of depression or mania (see Chapter 32 on affective illness), exacerbating the problem.

Hypoexpressive (Developmental Expressive Aprosodia)

Hypoexpressive children are stoic people. The young child resists peer interaction, continuing to play alone. This child often resists social activities, is labeled shy, is emotionally withdrawn, seems aloof, and is not generally affectionate, except possibly to his parents. The older child continues to reject others but is not rejected by others. These children are homebodies, and the severe hypoexpressive person is reclusive. This child is highly prone to depression and when in a depressive state becomes immobile and unable to leave home.

CHAPTER 27

MOTOR SKILLS

Motor skills are the development of efforts that produce movement. Poor motor co-ordination, clumsiness in the performance of complex motor tasks, and difficulties with age-appropriate motor activity are termed *developmental dyspraxias* or "the clumsy child syndrome." Neurologic examination fails to reveal any specific abnormal neurologic signs of motor system deficit. These children show remarkable improvement in the ability to perform complex motor tasks with increasing age.

Normal Development of Motor Skills

- Ages 6 to 7 months should be able to sit without support
- Ages 8 to 10 months should be able to crawl
- Ages 11 to 14 months should be able to walk
- Ages 22 to 28 months should be able to run
- Ages 2.5 to 4 years should be able to ride a tricycle using pedals
- Ages 3.5 to 4.5 years should be able to throw a ball
- Ages 4 to 5.5 years should be able to hop on one foot
- Ages 5.5 to 7 years should be able to skip
- Ages 5.5 to 7 years should be able to tie shoelaces
- Ages 5.5 to 7 years should be able to ride a bicycle

Assessing Motor Skills

- History of motor development from a knowledgeable parent, guardian, or caretaker
- Examination of the child for age-appropriate complex motor activity (see Normal Development)

Behaviors Associated With Deficits in Motor Skills

- Clumsiness without specific neurologic deficits of the motor system (ie, normal basic neurologic findings)

- The preschool-age child can have a history of delayed walking, remaining clumsy in running and in the use of utensils, and have difficulties buttoning, snapping, and tying

- They may dress backwards and place shoes on the wrong foot

- With increasing age, the child is delayed in learning to ride a tricycle and then a bicycle and in catching and throwing a ball

- These children are not athletically skillful but can enjoy sports, often being the last chosen for the team.

- Handwriting is often "messy"

- Frequent minor accidents often result from this clumsiness rather than on an impulsive basis

Clinical Picture of the Child With Deficits in Motor Skills (Dyspraxias)

The clumsy child is one who is delayed from early life in accomplishing motor milestones at the usual age. They often have frequent minor accidents not accounted for by impulsive behavior. They graduate into messy handwriting and often do not enjoy or are left out of team sports. Remarkable improvement occurs with increasing age into adolescence and young adulthood.

CHAPTER 28

RIGHT FRONTAL LOBE (PREFRONTAL) FUNCTION

Right frontal lobe (prefrontal) function involves the ability to follow the rules of society, compliance, obedience, volition (conscious or deliberate decision making), diligence (perseverance in a task), morality (ability to recognize the principles of right and wrong and to abide by the rules and regulations of society), and character ("the will").

Normal Development of Right Frontal Lobe (Prefrontal) Function

- By ages 3 to 5 years, children have highly developed volition, diligence, and morality

Assessing Right Frontal Lobe (Prefrontal) Function

- Interview with knowledgeable caretaker or guardian
- Observation and interview of the child

Behavior Associated With Deficits in Right Frontal Lobe (Prefrontal) Function

- Cruelty to pets and animals
- Little meaningful affection to others
- Long-standing noncompliance with ordinary rules and regulations
- Repeated play with matches (fire setting)
- Repeated stealing and cheating
- No remorse for unacceptable behavior

- Older individuals abuse the rights and dignity of others, break rules, and have recurrent encounters with legal authorities

Clinical Picture of Child With Deficits in Right Frontal Lobe (Prefrontal) Function (Character Disorder: Primary or Secondary to Affective Illness)

Young children will show no remorse and appear free of guilt. Abuse of pets and peers, playing with matches, lying to hurt other people, cheating in games (even when winning before cheating), and stealing for pleasure will be evident. They have little pain tolerance, do not conform to societal rules, and disregard the rights and feelings of others, leading to repeated legal difficulties.

CHAPTER 29

LEFT FRONTAL LOBE (PREFRONTAL) FUNCTION

Left frontal lobe (prefrontal) function involves rational thought.

Normal Development of Left Frontal Lobe (Prefrontal) Function

- The play of young children is characterized by purposeful fantasy and make-believe (delusions and hallucinations do not occur in normal development)

Assessing Left Frontal Lobe (Prefrontal) Function

- History from a knowledgeable parent, guardian, or caretaker
- Interview with the child asking about delusions and hallucinations
- If the child presents with delusions or hallucinations, the examiner must determine if the child is being commanded by the delusions or hallucination

Behaviors Associated With Deficits in Left Frontal Lobe (Prefrontal) Functions

- Speaking to imaginary playmates in a manner that interferes with social communication
- Speaking to one's own thoughts (delusions) in a question and answer format
- Evidence of distractibility with an interest in perceived objects that are not present
- Speaking in a manner not understandable to others but yet with clear diction

- Being frightened by perceived voices and/or objects that are not present
- Admitting to hearing voices known not to be real and/or visual images that the child knows not to be present

Clinical Picture of the Child With Deficits in Left Frontal Lobe (Prefrontal) Function (Thought Disorder: Primary or Secondary to Affective Illness)

Children or adolescents will appear to be avoiding certain areas, slapping space, picking on their skin, or turning around quite frequently, believing to hear their name being called "by a voice." When interviewed, they readily admit either to hearing voices that are calling their name, commanding them to perform an act, or stating negative comments about or to them. These auditory hallucinations are more frequent than visual hallucinations of misperceived objects. Those with deficits in the left frontal lobe have an impairment in clarity of thought with pronounced incapacitating delusions (a false belief [a belief that is invalid] and unresponsive to reason) and hallucinations (a perception of an external stimulus or object in the absence of such a stimulus or object).

Children and adolescents demonstrating impairment in the clarity of thought will be most often in a major depression with the bipolar feature of anger. Treating the associated affective illness will resolve these so-called "psychotic features" of the left frontal lobe. In older adolescents and adults, the primary disorder in clarity of thought is termed *schizophrenia*. The recognition of schizophrenia during childhood and young adolescent years remains questionable, but transient hallucinations and delusions are not uncommon during periods of affective illness including schizoaffective disorder.

CHAPTER 30

LOGIC, WIT, AND HUMOR

Logic

Logic is correct reasoning and the understanding of cause and effect.

Normal Development of Logic

- For simplistic events, logic is evident in young infants and possibly not fully developed until late middle age

Assessing Normal Logic

- Assessment of normal logic is subjective, based on the statement of the child's guardian and the child's ability to reason and understand cause and effect
- The clinician's observations of the child both in the free field and in structured settings

Behavior Associated With Deficits in Logic

- Inappropriate unreasonable behavior preventing meaningful interaction

Clinical Picture of the Child With Deficits in Logic

Alogic children show no meaningful interaction, prefer inanimate objects, and do not seem to understand the world about them even though they can appear otherwise normal and alert. Social judgment is lacking, as are meaningful appreciation, enjoyment, and expression. When logic is mildly impaired, pleasure can be evident in some social interaction, but difficulties remain in appreciating cause and effect, which is manifested as "explaining away" (rationalizing) causes of events, happenings, or feelings.

▌ Wit

Wit is the natural ability to perceive or to know.

Normal Development of Wit

- Wit is evident during young infancy and becomes a major variable in performance with increasing age

Assessing Normal Wit

- Assessment of normal wit is subjective, based on the statements of the guardian and the child's ability to perceive, adapt, and understand
- The clinician's observations of the child both in the free field and in structured settings

Behavior Associated With Deficits in Wit

- Children with limited wit have difficulty changing sets, adapting to or enjoying new situations, demonstrating judgment, and enjoying or appreciating a change or something that may be new
- These children can have difficulties appreciating variations and meaningful teasing by others, and words with various meanings may be misinterpreted
- This group of children often describes the environment in terms of colors rather than objects and events

Clinical Picture of the Child With Deficits in Wit

These children show poor judgment; are often stimulus dependent, being unable to plan or choose; do not seem to "roll with the punches"; are "black or white without shades of gray" in their thinking; have difficulty with meaningful laughter; and do not enjoy "fun and games." Despite a normal IQ, they display limited adaptive intelligence.

Humor

Humor is perceiving, appreciating, and adapting to situations.

Normal Development of Humor

* Humor is evident in young infants and is quite mature from toddler age onward

Assessing Humor

* Assessment of normal humor is subjective, based on the statements of the guardian and the child's ability to perceive, appreciate, and adapt to situations
* The clinician's observations of the child both in the free field and in structured settings

Behavior Associated With Deficits in Humor

* Difficulty tolerating change
* Requires sameness and learned structure to a level that impairs enjoyment
* Unable to "roll with the punches"
* Inability to enjoy immediate changes that might be enjoyable to others or to appreciate sudden dangers

Clinical Picture of the Child With Deficits in Humor

These children/adolescents are serious "little adults" who mandate routines, avoid change, and have difficulty with "fun and games."

CHAPTER 31

VIGILANCE

Vigilance is steady-state wakefulness/alertness (tonic arousal). It is required in order to maintain attention.

Normal Development of Vigilance

- Between ages 2 and 5 years, children have increasingly longer periods of vigilance, which is evident in increasing periods of wakefulness and fewer naps
- By ages 5 to 6 years, children do not take daytime naps and have extended periods of continuous mental and task performance with appropriate attention

Assessing Vigilance

- Observe the child during the interview for evidence of fidgeting, staring into space, shaking of legs, fingering objects, or arising from the chair to walk about the room and play with objects while being fully attentive to the conversation
- Observe the child or adolescent for yawning, stretching, or napping
- By report and observation, they have a unique temperament of kindness, caring, and affection and the inability to hold a grudge

Behavior Associated With Deficits in Vigilance

- Decreasing ability to sustain alertness, arousal, and wakefulness during continuous mental (or other task) performance (including reading and in lectures)
- Adolescents can complain of tiredness, drowsiness, sleepiness
- Yawning, stretching, sleepy-eyed appearance

- Falling asleep, excessive napping
- Motor restlessness
- Fidgeting
- Talkativeness
- Moving about
- Busyness
- Decreasing attention to activities
- Daydreaming
- Slow, delayed, or incomplete tasks
- Disorganized
- Avoidance of structured or repetitive activities
- Displays loss of interest in or complains that structured activities are dull, boring, monotonous, or uninteresting (or no longer interesting)
- Preferences for shifting activities that have random or irregular changes in schedule or activity (orderly randomization)
- Caring, compassionate, affectionate, kind temperament; unable to hold a grudge

Clinical Picture of the Child With Deficits in Vigilance (Primary Disorder of Vigilance)

These children want to and are able to perform a task but lose alertness and attention during such tasks and begin to daydream, fidget, move about, or fall asleep. They resist starting such tasks or resist activities that require repetition, knowing that they will lose attention (vigilance) with resultant discomfort and even failure in activities that they might master. These children are mildly busy (fiddling with pencils or other items in their desk, doodling, wiggling their feet, moving in their chairs, drumming their fingers, etc) and inattentive. They appear to be involved in other minor motor activities but when asked questions about what has been going on around them are able to respond correctly. They may talk to their neighbors or other classmates but are generally not disruptive to the class. They like to get up from their desks and sharpen pencils, get drinks of water, and perform other tasks that allow them to be mildly busy. They may stand next to their desk or squat in their chairs while trying to complete their work. These children enjoy classroom settings arranged in "centers" that permit them to go from one activity to another. They prefer busy environments rather than quiet, "be still" environments. Those children in whom the loss of vigilance is the primary problem are noted to be kind, affectionate, and angelic in nature. They are children who are attentive and alert when allowed to be busy.

These children fulfill many of the criteria for the diagnosis of attention-deficit hyperactive disorder (ADHD), inattentive form, and are often labeled as such.

Difficulties with vigilance can occur in isolation (primary form) and can also be associated with other conditions. Secondary causes of difficulty with vigilance include:

- Depression (sad, unhappy, lonely, hopeless, helpless feelings) (see Chapter 34)
- Learning disabilities (difficulties in reading, spelling, math, or other symbol skills)
- Narcolepsy (sleep attacks associated with cataplexy, hypnogogic hallucinations, and sleep paralysis)
- Sleep deprivation (including obstructive sleep apnea syndrome)
- Epilepsy (seizures)
- Drugs (eg, marijuana, cocaine)
- Medications (sedatives, antihistamines, antidepressants, anticonvulsants, neuroleptics)
- Toxins (poisons)
- Structural brain lesions (midbrain or right cerebral hemisphere)
- Hormonal or metabolic disorders (eg, hypothyroidism, hypoparathyroidism)

CHAPTER 32

DIAGNOSTIC SYNDROMES AND COMMON PATTERNS OF PRESENTATION

Table 2.   Summary of Specific Functions, Syndromes, and Anatomic Structures

Functions	Syndromes	Anatomic Structures
Reception of spoken words	Receptive dysphasia	Left Heschl's gyrus: middle part of the superior temporal gyrus
Inner speech	Auditory verbal agnosia, Wernicke's aphasia, pseudo-mental retardation, verbal dyslogia	Left visual association cortex
Word storage (inner vocabulary)	Word storage dysphasia	Left posterior parietal (prestriate) cortex
Specific word finding	Specific word finding dysphasia, dysnomia	Tract from left posterior parietal (prestriate) cortex to posterior portion of left superior temporal gyrus
Nominal recall	Nominal recall dysphasia	Mid portion of left posterior superior temporal gyrus
Word conduction	Word-conductive dysphasia	Left arcuate fasciculus
Word formulation	Broca-type aphasia	Left posterior inferior frontal gyrus
Storage of number graphemes	Dyssymbolia for numbers	Left anterior supramarginal gyrus
Recall of phonemes for numeric graphemes (arithmetic)	Phonemic recall dyscalculia	Anterior part of the anterior portion of left posterior superior temporal gyrus
Storage of letter graphemes	Dyssymbolia for letters	Left mid- and posterior supramarginal gyrus

Table 2. **Summary of Specific Functions, Syndromes, and Anatomic Structures (Continued)**

Functions	Syndromes	Anatomic Structures
Recall of phonemes for letter graphemes (spelling)	Phonemic recall dysphasia	Posterior part of the anterior portion of left posterior superior temporal gyrus
Decoding written words	Dyslexia	Left angular gyrus
Specific word recall after reading	Specific word finding after reading dysphasia, pseudo-reading comprehension dysphasia	Tract from left posterior parietal (prestriate) cortex to left angular gyrus
Orthography (graphic aspects of writing)	Orthographic dysgraphia	Inferior portion of right supramarginal gyrus
Global sequencing	Disorder of global sequencing	Right inferior parietal lobule and supramarginal gyrus
Events sequencing	Disorder of event sequencing	Right inferior parietal lobule
Symbol sequencing and symbol orientation	Developmental Gerstmann's syndrome	Superior portion of right supramarginal gyrus
Reception of nonverbal (gestural) prosody	Receptive visual aprosodia, visual dyslogia, pervasive developmental disorder	Right visual association cortex
Reception of verbal prosody	Receptive auditory (verbal) aprosodia	Right Heschl's gyrus: middle part of the superior temporal gyrus
Conduction of nonverbal (gestural) prosody	Conductive gestural dysprosodia	Tract from right visual association cortex and right parietal (prestriate) cortex to right anterior inferior frontal gyrus
Conduction of verbal prosody	Conductive verbal dysprosodia	Tract (fasciculus) from right Heschl's to right posterior inferior frontal

Table 2. Summary of Specific Functions, Syndromes, and Anatomic Structures (Continued)

Functions	Syndromes	Anatomic Structures
Formulation of nonverbal (gestural) prosody	Ross-type expressive gestural dysprosodia	Right anterior inferior frontal gyrus
Formulation of verbal prosody	Ross-type expressive verbal dysprosodia	Right posterior inferior frontal gyrus (Ross's area)
Retrieval of correct prosody		
Hyperexpression	Asperger's syndrome, expressive dysprosodia	Posterior portion of right posterior parietal (prestriate) cortex
Hypoexpression	Developmental expressive aprosodia	Anterior portion of right posterior parietal (prestriate) cortex
Motor skills	Developmental clumsiness/ dyspraxias	Right superior parietal lobule
Volition, diligence, and morality	Character disorder (primary or secondary to affective illness)	Right orbital frontal cortex
Clarity of thought	Thought disorder (primary or secondary to affective illness)	Left orbital frontal cortex
Vigilance	Primary disorder of vigilance	Right inferior parietal lobule (plus parts of right supramarginal gyrus, prestriate cortex, and superior parietal lobule)
Mood and affect	Depression	Right posterior temporal cortex, posterior parietal (prestriate) cortex, and inferior parietal lobule
	Mania	Left mesial temporal cortex (entorhinal cortex)

Table 3.   Common Patterns of Presentation

	Nominal Recall Dysphasia	Orthographic Dysgraphia	Orthographic Dysgraphia With Phonemic Recall Dysphasia for Letters (Spelling)	Orthographic Dysgraphia With Limited Global Sequencing With or Without Phonemic (Letters and/or Numbers) and/or Nominal Recall Dysphasia	Orthographic Dysgraphia With Phonemic Recall Dysphasia for Both Letters and Numbers	Orthographic Dysgraphia With Phonemic and Nominal Recall Dysphasia
Chapter 3 Reception of Spoken Words						
Chapter 4 Inner Speech						
Chapter 5 Word Storage (Inner Vocabulary)						
Chapter 6 Specific Word Finding						
Chapter 7 Nominal Recall	XX			XX		XX
Chapter 8 Word Conduction						
Chapter 9 Word Formulation						
Chapter 10 Storage of Number Graphemes						
Chapter 11 Recall of Phonemes for Number Graphemes				XX	XX	XX
Chapter 12 Storage of Letter Graphemes						
Chapter 13 Recall of Phonemes for Letter Graphemes			XX	XX	XX	XX
Chapter 14 Reading and Reading Comprehension						
Chapter 15 Orthography (Graphic Aspects of Writing)		XX	XX	XX	XX	XX

Table 3.   Common Patterns of Presentation (Continued)

	Nominal Recall Dysphasia	Orthographic Dysgraphia	Orthographic Dysgraphia With Phonemic Recall Dysphasia for Letters (Spelling)	Orthographic Dysgraphia With Limited Global Sequencing With or Without Phonemic (Letters and/or Numbers) and/or Nominal Recall Dysphasia	Orthographic Dysgraphia With Phonemic Recall Dysphasia for Both Letters and Numbers	Orthographic Dysgraphia With Phonemic and Nominal Recall Dysphasia
Chapter 16 Global Sequencing				XX		
Chapter 17 Events Sequencing						
Chapter 18 Symbol Sequencing and Symbol Orientation						
Chapter 20 Reception of Nonverbal (Gestural) Prosody						
Chapter 21 Reception of Verbal Prosody						
Chapter 22 Conduction of Nonverbal Prosody						
Chapter 23 Conduction of Verbal Prosody						
Chapter 24 Formulation of Nonverbal (Gestural) Prosody						
Chapter 25 Formulation of Verbal Prosody						
Chapter 26 Retrieval of Correct Verbal and Gestural Prosody						
Chapter 27 Motor Skills						
Chapter 28 Right Frontal Lobe Function						
Chapter 29 Left Frontal Lobe Function						

Table 3.   Common Patterns of Presentation (Continued)

	Diffuse Symbol Language Disorder (Dyslexia Plus)	Hyperprosody With or Without Dysgraphia and Phonemic Recall Dysphasia for Numbers and Limited Sequencing	Hypoprosody With or Without Dysgraphia With Phonemic Recall Dysphasia for Numbers and Limited Sequencing	Aphasia	Gerstmann's Syndrome (With or Without Disturbance of Event or Global Sequencing) and Graphomotor Writing (Spatial Relations)	Gerstmann's Syndrome With Phonemic Recall Dysphasia for Either or Both Number and Letter Phonemes and/or Nominal Recall Dysphasia
Chapter 3 Reception of Spoken Words	XX			XX		
Chapter 4 Inner Speech				XX		
Chapter 5 Word Storage (Inner Vocabulary)				XX		
Chapter 6 Specific Word Finding	XX			XX		
Chapter 7 Nominal Recall	XX			XX		XX
Chapter 8 Word Conduction				XX		
Chapter 9 Word Formulation				XX		
Chapter 10 Storage of Number Grapheme	XX					
Chapter 11 Recall of Phonemes for Number Graphemes	XX	XX	XX	XX		XX
Chapter 12 Storage of Letter Graphemes	XX					
Chapter 13 Recall of Phonemes for Letter Graphemes	XX			XX		XX
Chapter 14 Reading and Reading Comprehension	XX					
Chapter 15 Orthography (Graphic Aspects of Writing)	XX	XX	XX		XX	XX

Table 3.   Common Patterns of Presentation (Continued)

	Diffuse Symbol Language Disorder (Dyslexia Plus)	Hyperprosody With or Without Dysgraphia and Phonemic Recall Dysphasia for Numbers and Limited Sequencing	Hypoprosody With or Without Dysgraphia With Phonemic Recall Dysphasia for Numbers and Limited Sequencing	Aphasia	Gerstmann's Syndrome (With or Without Disturbance of Event or Global Sequencing) and Graphomotor Writing (Spatial Relations)	Gerstmann's Syndrome With Phonemic Recall Dysphasia for Either or Both Number and Letter Phonemes and/or Nominal Recall Dysphasia
Chapter 16 Global Sequencing		XX	XX		XX	XX
Chapter 17 Events Sequencing					XX	XX
Chapter 18 Symbol Sequencing and Symbol Orientation	XX				XX	XX
Chapter 20 Reception of Nonverbal (Gestural) Prosody						
Chapter 21 Reception of Verbal Prosody						
Chapter 22 Conduction of Nonverbal Prosody		XX	XX			
Chapter 23 Conduction of Verbal Prosody		XX	XX			
Chapter 24 Formulation of Nonverbal (Gestural) Prosody		XX	XX			
Chapter 25 Formulation of Verbal Prosody		XX	XX			
Chapter 26 Retrieval of Correct Verbal and Gestural Prosody		XX	XX			
Chapter 27 Motor Skills						
Chapter 28 Right Frontal Lobe Function						
Chapter 29 Left Frontal Lobe Function						

CHAPTER 33

TREATMENT FOR LEARNING DEFICITS

Table 4.   Treatment for Deficits by Chapter

Deficits	Treatment
Chapter 3 Reception of Spoken Words	Speak clearly to child's eyes with good diction and appropriate gestures Repeat statements and requests as needed
Chapter 4 Inner Speech	Limit (avoid) verbal directions, commands, or requests Promote the use of gestures and pictures for communication and interaction Use words in sync with their pictorial representation
Chapter 5 Word Storage (Inner Vocabulary)	Encourage a "see and do" environment and method of communication Use gestures for communication Provide words "in sync" with pictures and gestures for the development of vocabulary Offer multiple choice in verbal communication using very common words
Chapter 6 Specific Word Finding	Retrieve words through multiple-choice formats Encourage nonverbal communication Use appropriate gestures and animations in association with words
Chapter 7 Nominal Recall	Offer multiple-choice testing Use multiple choice in daily communication
Chapter 8 Word Conduction	Speech boards and other vocalization technology Provide simple pictures that show children doing everyday activities that the child can use to point to what he or she is trying to express
Chapter 9 Word Formulation	Speech boards and other vocalization technology Simple pictures that show children doing everyday activities that the child can use to point to what he or she is trying to express

Table 4.   Treatment for Deficits by Chapter (Continued)

Deficits	Treatment
Chapter 10 Storage of Number Graphemes	Abacuses, counting rods, calculators Use matching formats for numeric language tasks
Chapter 11 Recall of Phonemes for Number Graphemes (Arithmetic)	Use age-appropriate number concepts and principles Abacuses, counting rods, and calculators Instruct through multiple choice Test by multiple choice
Chapter 12 Storage of Letter Graphemes	Movies, computers, lectures, and books on tape Listen to good readers read age-appropriate material Use matching formats for the letter tasks
Chapter 13 Recall of Phonemes for Letter Graphemes (Spelling)	Encourage the child to look at the word while hearing the word spoken Test spelling by multiple-choice format Use spelling aid such as *The Bad Speller's Dictionary* Use secretary with good spelling ability Computer with word processing and spellcheck software
Chapter 14 Reading and Reading Comprehension	Listen to "good readers" read age-appropriate material while eyeing the printed page Use talking books, tapes, movies Read silently for meaning, not aloud Test orally and provide reader and recorder for written tests Use reading aids such as highlighted texts, Cliff Notes, abstracts, and synopses Read only the salient material, knowing what is to be learned prior to reading such material Build reading vocabulary through written words in sync with their pictorial representation
Chapter 15 Orthography (Graphic Aspects of Writing)	Computer for writing Secretary Dictating equipment Oral testing or multiple-choice formats Pictorial systems for self-reminding
Chapter 16 Global Sequencing	Offer one small task at a time Divide large tasks into several smaller tasks and offer one at a time

Table 4. Treatment for Deficits by Chapter (Continued)

Deficits	Treatment
	Provide systems of reminders including pictorial systems for self-reminders
Chapter 17 Events Sequencing	Associate with a well-organized "director of affairs" Provide pictorial systems for self-reminders
Chapter 18 Symbol Sequencing and Symbol Orientation	Calculator Computers Multiple-choice formats Offer one task at a time
Chapter 20 Reception of Nonverbal (Gestural) Prosody	Use words with appropriate gestures rather than gestures alone when communicating commands, requests, or statements. Do not depend on the gestures alone for understanding.
Chapter 21 Reception of Verbal Prosody	Use appropriate gestures in association with words relying on the gesture for understanding
Chapter 22 Conduction of Nonverbal (Gestural) Prosody	Allow child to verbally express himself Attend to what the child says rather than the gesture or animation
Chapter 23 Conduction of Verbal Prosody	Allow child to gesture or put into action Attend to what child does (and gestures) rather than tone of speech
Chapter 24 Formulation of Nonverbal (Gestural) Prosody	Allow child to verbally express himself Attend to what the child says and speech tones rather than the gesture or animation
Chapter 25 Formulation of Verbal Prosody	Allow child to gesture or put into action Attend to what child does (and gestures) rather than tone of speech
Chapter 26 Retrieval of Correct	Appropriate models to tone down the *hyper*prosodic child without being critical

Table 4. Treatment for Deficits by Chapter (Continued)

Deficits	Treatment
Verbal and Gestural Prosody	Offer appropriate speech tones, gestures, and animations for the *hypo*prosodic child to avoid the stoic or monotone expression
Chapter 27 Motor Skills	"Will improve with age" attitude Avoid undue practice Offer games and activities of choice Push carts, four-wheel carts, and training wheels until balance develops for bicycle riding Avoid demeaning feedback
Chapter 28 Right Frontal Lobe Function	Supervision, protection, structured controlled activities Avoid unsupervised free-time activities
Chapter 29 Left Frontal Lobe Function	Identify, recognize, and treat the underlying affective illness (bipolar disorder)
Chapter 30 Logic, Wit, and Humor	Avoid ambivalence Avoid teasing, demeaning interactions Assist with planning by explaining cause in relationship to happenings Prepare the individual for changes and for the event Offer meaning to the occurrence with preparation for the occurrences Leave "nothing for granted," offer interpretations without choices
Chapter 31 Vigilance	Reading should be limited to only the salient material, knowing what is to be learned before reading such material Allow minor busyness (fidgets, dawdling, manipulative hand play) Provide frequent mini breaks in prolonged tasks Extended time on major tests with mini breaks In sum, stay busy to be alert, to learn, and to perform Stimulant medication when indicated (see Chapter 36)

Table 4. Treatment for Deficits by Chapter (Continued)

Deficits	Treatment
Chapter 34 Depression	Removal of inappropriate stresses especially in the school setting; use bypass/compensatory strategies for successful performance (see above and Table 5) Cognitive coaching Appropriate medications (see Chapter 36) Recognition and treatment of adult family members
Chapter 34 Mania	Removal of inappropriate stresses (see above in depression) Cognitive coaching Appropriate medications (see Chapter 36) Recognition and treatment of adult family members

Table 5.   Treatment for Common Patterns of Presentation

Nominal recall dysphasia	Offer multiple-choice testing format
Orthographic dysgraphia	Computer for writing Secretary Dictating equipment Oral testing Multiple-choice testing format
Orthographic dysgraphia with phonemic recall dysphasia for letters (spelling)	Look at the word while hearing the word spoken Use spelling aids such as *The Bad Speller's Dictionary* Secretary Computer with appropriate software including spellcheck function and thesaurus Multiple-choice spelling tests
Orthographic dysgraphia with limited global sequencing, with or without phonemic (letters and/or numbers) and/or nominal recall dysphasia	Computer for writing Secretary Multiple-choice testing format Calculator Offer one small task at a time or divide larger tasks into several mini tasks Provide reminders of tasks; avoid nagging Use pictorial systems for self-reminding of tasks, chores, and events Offer all testing using an untimed format
Orthographic dysgraphia with phonemic recall dysphasia for both letters and numbers	Computer with appropriate software including spellcheck function and thesaurus Multiple-choice testing format Calculator
Orthographic dysgraphia with phonemic and nominal recall dysphasia	Computer with appropriate software including spellcheck function and thesaurus Multiple-choice testing format Calculator
Diffuse symbol language disorder (dyslexia plus)	Computer with appropriate software Use talking books, tapes, and movies Listen to good readers read age-appropriate material Read silently for meaning, not aloud

Table 5.   Treatment for Common Patterns of Presentation (Continued)

	Test orally and provide reader and recorder for written tests
	Use reading aids such as highlighted texts and Cliff Notes
	Multiple-choice testing format, including spelling
	Calculator
Hyperdysprosody plus with or without dysgraphia and phonemic recall dysphasia for numbers and limited sequencing	Avoid over-responding to child's hyperexpressivity
	Be an appropriate model for expression
	Provide appropriate models for expression
	Calculator
	Offer one task at a time
	Computer with appropriate software
	Multiple-choice formats
	Added time as needed on standardized tests
Hypodysprosody plus with or without dysgraphia, with phonemic recall dysphasia for numbers and limited sequential order	Ask questions as needed to ensure understanding
	Avoid unneeded repetition in communication
	Provide appropriate models for expression
	Calculator
	Offer one task at a time
	Computer with appropriate software
	Multiple-choice formats
	Added time as needed on standardized tests
Developmental aphasia	Speak clearly to the child's eyes
	Respond appropriately to the child's gestures while offering the word for the gesture
	Avoid correcting the child's word conduction
	Retrieve specific words through multiple-choice format of communication
	Avoid having child repeat words
	Offer speech board (talk boards) using age-appropriate words
Pseudo-reading comprehension dysnomia	Examine reading comprehension by nonverbal performance tasks ("putting learned information into action")
	Test and retrieve specific information using multiple-choice format, thus bypassing the dysnomia

CHAPTER 34

Affect and Mood (Depression, Manic-Depressive Disease, and Other Bipolar Disorders)

Affective illness is a disorder of mood and feelings. Affective illness is a genetic disorder that presents with a variety of symptoms (patterns) at various ages. The family history (three generations) can be the "familial affective disorder" (only positive for affective illness) or "mixed-type family history" (positive for early-onset alcoholism, drug abuse, Briquet's syndrome, schizophrenia [thought disorder], and/or sociopathy).

Normal Development of Affect and Mood

- By ages 2 to 3 years, stability of moods is evident and cessation of inappropriate periods of crying and separation anxiety is noted

- Although people at all ages can feel anger, young children by age 3 years already learn not to show excessive or inappropriate anger or not to be abusive to others

- Children at ages 2 to 3 years without affective illness report "happy" feelings, good self-worth, and enjoyment in their activities

Assessing Affective Illness

- Obtain a detailed history from a knowledgeable guardian

- Obtain a family history (three generations) addressing patterns of mood disorders, alcohol, drug abuse, Briquet's syndrome, schizophrenia, and sociopathy

- Perform a closed-ended, semi-structured interview of the child

- Ask the child, "Can I ask you some very personal questions?" A sampling of questions follows: "Are you having mostly good, mixed, or bad days in your feelings?" "On these mixed or bad days, are you having feelings of sadness, unhappiness, or grouchiness?" "On these mixed or bad days, are you having good or bad feelings about yourself?" "Is it so bad that you go off to your room and cry?" "Are you able to have fun on these mixed or bad days?"

- Ask about death wishes, suicidal thoughts and plans, difficulty with sleep, loss of energy and usual interests, and difficulties with attention and concentration

- Ask the child or adolescent to rate himself or herself using a scale of 1 to 10, demarcated with the following descriptions: 1 = "the pits"; 3 = "no good, too many mixed and bad days that are causing problems"; 5 = "halfway, not too bad, but not good enough"; 7 = "some ups and downs but no real problems; I am feeling and doing fine"; and 10 = "perfect, no problems at all"

- Depression by patient self-report can be assessed with the Weinberg Depression Scale for Children and Adolescents (WDSCA, Pro-Ed, Austin, TX). The Weinberg Screening Affective Scale-Short Form (WSAS-SF) (Table 6) can also be used. Both scales require a fourth-grade reading ability and only a few minutes to complete.

Clinical Picture of the Child With Disorders of Affect and Mood

The hypomanic/manic symptomatology of affective illness is prominent during toddler and preschool years with depressive symptomatology becoming more evident during elementary school years with or without the continuation of the hypomanic/manic symptoms. Major depressive disorder occurs at all

Table 6.   Weinberg Screening Affective Scale-Short Form (WSAS-SF)

Instructions

We would like to ask you some serious and very important questions. We want to know how you feel about yourself. If you agree with the statement, circle yes. If you do not agree with the statement, circle no. We consider these questions and your answers very important.

1.	I will try to give my honest feelings on these questions.	Yes	No
2.	I can't concentrate on my work.	Yes	No
3.	I feel lonely too much of the time.	Yes	No
4.	I don't want to go to school anymore.	Yes	No
5.	It seems like some part of my body always hurts me.	Yes	No
6.	People are always talking about me when I'm not there.	Yes	No
7.	I have too many bad moods.	Yes	No
8.	I don't have fun playing with my friends anymore.	Yes	No
9.	It's hard to fall asleep and that bothers me.	Yes	No
10.	I can't do anything right.	Yes	No
11.	I feel too tired to play.	Yes	No
12.	I daydream too much in school.	Yes	No
13.	I think a lot about killing myself.	Yes	No
14.	My answers are how I have been feeling most of the time.	Yes	No
15.	These answers represent my honest feelings.	Yes	No

To score the WSAS-SF, we use the following: questions 1, 14, and 15 must be "yes" to consider the responses reliable; using questions 2 through 13, 0–3 "yes" responses = negative for depression, 4–6 "yes" responses = possibly depressed, and 7–12 "yes" responses = depression until proven otherwise.

ages, becoming more prevalent during early adolescence, often associated with the bipolar feature of hostile anger. The well-recognized patterns of affective illness commonly seen in children and adolescents are as follows:

- *Mania* is characterized by euphoria (denial of any problems), rages, hostile anger that persists for more than 1 to 2 weeks, and malfunctioning generally in all three environments (school, home, and play). Oppositional/defiant behavior and incapacitating compulsions are symptomatic of mania.

- *Hypomania* is chronic hyperactivity with associated inappropriate cheerfulness, silliness, intrusiveness, and disruptive behavior. Often with increasing age there are symptoms of racing thoughts, push of speech, inappropriate provocative sexual behaviors, and irritable moods, with a decreased need for sleep. Night owl (not ready for sleep) insomnia is common.

- *Cyclothymia* is chronic, long-standing (greater than 1 year) hypomanic/hyperactivity with moment to moment and day to day (mixed days) manic and depressive moods and feelings with no prolonged well states and no discrete periods of depression or mania.

- *Juvenile rapid cycling bipolar disorder* is characterized by chronic, long-standing mixed days of both manic and depressive moods and feelings with no prolonged well states but freedom from chronic hypomanic/hyperactivity and no discrete periods of depression or mania.

- *Dysthymia* is long-standing (greater than 1 year) depressive moods and feelings with variable vegetative symptoms of insomnia, low energy, decreased interest, and affection that fluctuate in the pattern of mixed days with occasional "all bad days" and with no prolonged, stable (well) states. However, the child/adolescent functions in all environments.

- *Dysthymia with bipolar features* is dysthymia with brief, recurrent "moments" (periods) of hostile anger.

- *Depression* is defined as a discrete period persisting for more than 2 weeks of dysphoric moods and feelings characterized by both statements and appearance of sadness, unhappiness, pessimism, loneliness, and low self-worth;

vegetative symptoms of insomnia, change in appetite and weight, low energy, less affection, and/or fatigue; and, not uncommonly, with anhedonia and suicidal ideation. Children/adolescents in an episode of depression will be malfunctioning in one or more environments.

- *Manic-depressive disease* (classic bipolar disorder) is characterized by episodes of depression persisting for more than 2 weeks with manic episodes persisting for 1 or more weeks interspersed with months or years of stable ("well") periods.

Age seems to be a significant variable in the phenotypic presentation of affective illness. Young children (ages 1–5 years) tend to manifest prominent hypomanic-manic symptomatology. Depressive symptomatology becomes more prominent in later childhood years and in adolescents. However, dysthymia and depression occur in all age groups. Probably more common is the dysthymic or cyclothymic patterns progressing from a young age to an episode of depression during adolescence with or without a classic period of mania.

Clinical Picture of Depression

Symptoms

- Dysphoric moods/feelings: statements or appearance of sadness, unhappiness, loneliness, frustration, anxiety/worry, hopelessness, helplessness, and/or pessimism; irritable, easily annoyed; hypersensitive with ease of crying; negative and difficult to please

- Self-deprecatory ideation; feelings of being worthless, useless, dumb, stupid, ugly, guilty; beliefs of persecution; death wishes; suicidal thoughts; suicidal attempts

- Aggressive behavior (agitation); difficult to get along with; quarrelsome; disrespectful of authority; belligerent, hostile, agitated; excessive fighting or sudden anger

- Sleep disturbance, initial insomnia, restless sleep, terminal insomnia, difficulty awakening in morning
- Change in school performance; frequent complaints from teachers ("daydreaming," "poor concentration," "poor memory"); loss of usual work effort in school subjects; loss of usual interest in nonacademic school activities; many incomplete classroom assignments; much incomplete homework; a drop in usual grades; finds homework difficult
- Diminished socialization, less group participation, less friendly, less outgoing, socially withdrawing, loss of usual social interests
- Change in attitude toward school, does not enjoy school activities, does not want or refuses to attend school
- Somatic complaints; nonmigraine headaches, abdominal pain, muscle aches or pains, other somatic concerns or complaints
- Loss of usual energy, loss of usual personal interests or pursuits (other than school, eg, hobbies), decreased activity level, mental and/or physical fatigue, loss of the ability to anticipate and/or experience pleasure (anhedonia)
- Unusual change in appetite and/or weight, anorexia or polyphagia, unusual weight change in past 4 months

Criteria

Combining the original criteria for depression in children (Weinberg et al.[1]) and the *DSM-IV*,[3] children and adolescents in a depressive episode will manifest dysphoric moods and feelings (with or without anhedonia) and self-deprecation plus four or more of the remaining eight depressive symptoms. These symptoms must be present for more than 2 weeks, a change from the individual's usual self, and associated with malfunctioning in one or more of the three environments (home, school, and play).

Children with depression appear isolated, unhappy, and irritable and lose interest in things that used to be enjoyable. They have a pallor with dark circles under their eyes, seem lethargic, and have latency to respond to questions asked. They have difficulty separating from parents or other significant caregivers. They complain of headaches, stomach aches, or muscle aches. These children have difficulty initiating sleep at their normal bedtime and lay in bed feeling sleepy but unable to go to sleep. They have awakenings in the middle of the night or awaken early in the morning and are unable to return to sleep. They can return to wetting the bed. These children experience a change in energy level and in appetite (either an increase or decrease). They express feelings of being hopeless or helpless. Children with depression have difficulty experiencing or anticipating pleasure and thus can be reluctant to go to the activities that in the past they looked forward to attending (anhedonia). These children start feeling and expressing negative feelings about themselves, such as "I'm ugly," "I'm stupid," and "I'm no good." They state that they have feelings of no longer wanting to live and plans to hurt themselves in some way (suicidal ideation). The child's depressed moods and feelings are associated with malfunctioning in one or more environments: home, school, and/or play.

Neurologic examination will often demonstrate a left hemi-motor syndrome (Figure 8). The most common findings are dishing or spooning of the left hand at the metacarpal phalangeal joint when the arm is held extended in front of the body with the fingers outstretched and clumsy rapid alternating movements of the left arm/hand. A slight tremor of the left arm/hand is also common. When lying supine, as if to fall asleep, the left leg/foot will be externally rotated. There can even be more brisk left-sided tendon reflexes and a left Babinski reflex. These findings show remarkable improvement when the depression lifts but may not fully disappear. In

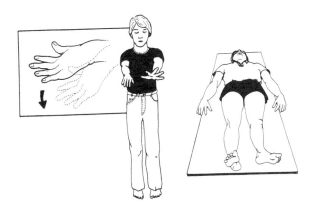

Figure 8. Hemimotor syndrome: The child is told to stand with eyes closed and arms outstretched in front with palms of the hands facing the floor. Normally, the arms will be symmetrically positioned and the hands will be flat. Starting from the symmetric position, the abnormal posturing will become evident as one hand (in this example, the left hand) bends at the wrist toward the floor (see insert) and the fingers extend backward to make the top surface of the hand concave (like the end of a spoon—hence the term "spooning"). The child's leg position at rest is evaluated by having the child lie flat with the head straight, arms at sides, eyes closed, and legs spread slightly apart and relaxed. The legs ordinarily should be symmetric (usually the toes are directed slightly outward, but occasionally they can be straight or turned slightly inward); marked external rotation of the one leg (foot and leg rotated outward) compared with the other leg is abnormal.

adults with dysthymia, cyclothymia, and those who have had recurrent periods of major depression, these findings can be permanent.

Clinical Picture of Mania

Symptoms

- Euphoria: denial of problems or illness, inappropriate feelings of well-being, inappropriate cheerfulness, giddiness and silliness

- Irritability and/or agitation, hostile anger: belligerence and destructiveness, and antisocial behavior that is unusual for the person (ie, out of character)

- Hyperactivity, "motor driven," intrusiveness, disruptive/interruptive behavior

- Push of speech (may become unintelligible), garrulousness, "motor mouth"

- Flight of ideas, "racing thoughts"

- Grandiosity (can be delusional)

- Sleep disturbance (decreased sleep and unusual sleep pattern)

- Distractibility (short attention span), inattentiveness, unable to maintain focus when alert (inability to concentrate)

- Provocative sexual activity, heightened sexual awareness and/or interest

Criteria

Children and adolescents in a manic episode will manifest either euphoria and/or irritable moods (often hostile) with three or more of the remaining six symptoms (Weinberg & Brumback,[2] *DSM-IV*[3]). These symptoms must be present for at least 1 week, must be different from the individual's usual self, and must produce malfunctioning at home, school, and/or play.

Children with mania or hypomania appear active, busy, and on the go. Their hyperactivity can be mental, verbal, motor, and/or sexual. They can make inappropriate comments and gestures.

Their thoughts rapidly change from one to another. They speak very rapidly. They have temper fits and rages, becoming "out of control." The anger of mania is hostile anger and can become homicidal. The child with mania will deny having any problems. Anger can come and go very quickly and be initiated by variable things at different times. Following a show of hostile anger, these children express remorse and then a depressed period. Their behaviors can be very disruptive at school, at home, and in play environments because of their hyperactivity and their quick anger. When confronted, these children can become aggressive, both verbally and physically, to others. During a manic episode, they are impulsive, with poor judgment, and can be abusive to people and property, with no remorse and denying any problems (euphoria), which is a change from their usual self. Problematic oppositional, defiant behavior and obsessive-compulsive behavior can also be symptomatic of mania, particularly in young children.

Neurologic findings in mania will consist of a right hemimotor syndrome. The findings of the right limbs are the same as reported above in the left limbs for depression. Pure mania will demonstrate only a right hemimotor syndrome, but, more commonly, these motor findings will be evident in all four limbs, suggesting a bipolar affective illness with prominent manic symptoms.

References

1. Weinberg WA, Rutman J, Sullivan L, et al. Depression in children referred to an educational diagnostic center: diagnosis and treatment. J Pediatr 1973;83:1065–1072.
2. Weinberg WA, Brumback RA. Mania in childhood: case studies and literature review. Am J Dis Child 1976;130:380–385.
3. Diagnostic and Statistical Manual of Mental Disorders. 4th Ed. Washington, DC: American Psychiatric Association, 1994.

CHAPTER 35

TREATMENT PROTOCOL FOR AFFECTIVE ILLNESS

Treatment of affective illness is both simplistic and complex. Recognizing the present pattern of the affective illness, whether the symptoms are pure depression, only mania, or mixed, and the developmental history of the patterns of the affective illness over time in the individual are most important.

Simultaneous to the use of medication (or in some cases preceding trials of medication), the individual's environment must be changed to reduce inappropriate stress. The home environment should be stable and rewarding with positive and nurturing interaction. An affectively ill parent or guardian must also be recognized and offered appropriate treatment. For learning disabilities, bypass compensatory strategies and assistive technologies must be provided in regular, mainstream classes with usual peers as colleagues (see Chapter 33). Remediation, more time on task, and excessive homework (or any homework) should be avoided. Pursuit of the individual's assets, talents, and creativities should be encouraged, with good support and leadership. Battles, confrontations, and punishment of the depressed child should be minimized. Cognitive coaching on a "mini" daily basis is also useful, that is, encouraging the individual to use intelligence to override emotions—having actions dictate feelings and not allowing feelings to cause actions.

Prior to trials of medication, physical and neurologic examinations are indicated to rule out any other medical disorders, and a premedication electrocardiogram is obtained. Chemistries, including a thyroid profile and urinalysis, are only obtained if indicated by history and/or physical findings.

Parents and child or adolescent can benefit from ongoing formal psychological management using a cognitive, educational, interpersonal approach.

CHAPTER 36

MEDICATION

Antidepressant pharmacotherapy is presented in Table 7.

Antimanic pharmacotherapy is presented in Table 8.

Table 7.   Antidepressant Pharmacotherapy

Medication	Dosage Range	Serum Level (ng/mL)	Indications	Contraindications	Potential Adverse Effects
Amitriptyline	Children 1–3 mg/kg/d (up to 5 mg/kg/d if monitored) Adolescents 100–200 mg/d	100–250 (sum of amitriptyline plus nortriptyline)	Depression in non-obese preadolescents, or with a history of "pure familial" type of affective disorder Migraine Enuresis Cyclic vomiting	Obesity Excessive daytime sleepiness History of paroxysmal atrial tachycardia or other cardiac conduction disturbances Liver or renal disease unless dose and serum levels can be closely monitored	Induction or promotion of mania Atropinic side effects Mild tremor Worsening of depressive symptoms Increased appetite and excess weight gain Excessive daytime sleepiness Rash EKG evidence of cardiac conduction changes
Bupropion	Children 37.5–150 mg/d in 2 divided dosages Adolescents 75–150 mg bid or tid	10–30 or 50–100, depending on laboratory studies	Depression Bipolar type II	Significantly under-weight or with anorexia History of paroxysmal atrial tachycardia or other cardiac conduction disturbances Liver or renal disease (closely monitored) Active seizure disorder Liver disease Anorexia	Seizures Induction of liver enzymes Rash

Table 7. Antidepressant Pharmacotherapy (Continued)

Medication	Dosage Range	Serum Level (ng/mL)	Indications	Contraindications	Potential Adverse Effects
Citalopram	Children and adolescents 10–40 mg/d (qam)	Not available	Depression	Same as sertraline	Same as sertraline
Desipramine (a metabolite of imipramine)	Children 1–3 mg/kg/d (up to 5 mg/kg/d if monitored) Adolescents 100–200 mg/d	50–300	Depression	Same as nortriptyline	Same as imipramine plus insomnia
Doxepin	Children 1–3 mg/kg/d Adolescents 100–200 mg/d	75–200	Depression in non-obese children and adolescents with prominent anxiety, phobias, and somatic symptoms	Same as amitriptyline	Same as amitriptyline, except infrequently induces or promotes mania

Table 7. Antidepressant Pharmacotherapy (Continued)

Medication	Dosage Range	Serum Level (ng/mL)	Indications	Contraindications	Potential Adverse Effects
Fluoxetine	Children 10–20 mg qam Adolescents 20–40 mg qam	100–900 (combined)	Depression OCD Migraine	Significantly underweight or with anorexia History of paroxysmal atrial tachycardia or other cardiac conduction disturbances Liver or renal disease (closely monitored) Prominent anger Excessive daytime sleepiness	Decreased appetite and excess weight loss Confusion Incoordination Insomnia Induction or promotion of mania Rash Akathisia Nervousness Gastrointestinal symptoms Hypovigilance
Imipramine	Children 1–3 mg/kg/d (up to 5 mg/kg/d if monitored) Adolescents 100–200 mg/d	150–250 (sum of imipramine plus desipramine)	Depression Migraine Enuresis	Significantly underweight or with anorexia History of paroxysmal atrial tachycardia or other cardiac conduction disturbances Liver or renal disease unless dose and serum levels can be closely monitored	Induction or promotion of mania Atropinic side effects Mild tremor Worsening of depression Decreased appetite and excess weight loss Excessive daytime sleepiness Rash EKG evidence of cardiac conduction changes Hypertension

Table 7. Antidepressant Pharmacotherapy (Continued)

Medication	Dosage Range	Serum Level (ng/mL)	Indications	Contraindications	Potential Adverse Effects
Maprotiline	Adolescents 75–300 mg/d	200–600	Alternate drug for depression in obese adolescents or with excessive daytime sleepiness	Same as imipramine	Same as imipramine, plus insomnia
Nefazodone	50–300 mg/d	Not available	Depression Anxiety	Same as trazodone	Dizziness Sedation
Nortriptyline (a metabolite of amitriptyline)	Children 1–3 mg/kg/d Adolescents 50–150 mg/d	50–150	Depression	History of paroxysmal atrial tachycardia or other cardiac conduction disturbances Liver or renal disease unless dose and serum levels can be closely monitored	Same as amitriptyline except with less effect on appetite and weight "Therapeutic window" in which subtherapeutic dosages worsen depression
Paroxetine	Children 10–30 mg qam Adolescents 10–40 mg qam	Not available	Depression Social anxiety/phobia OCD	Same as fluoxetine	Same as fluoxetine Fatigue/drowsiness Abnormal ejaculation/orgasm

Table 7. Antidepressant Pharmacotherapy (Continued)

Medication	Dosage Range	Serum Level (ng/mL)	Indications	Contraindications	Potential Adverse Effects
Protriptyline	Children 5–10 mg bid or tid* Adolescents 5–15 mg bid or tid*	70–260	Secondary drug for depression in association with excessive daytime sleepiness (the primary disorder of vigilance)	Same as nortriptyline	Induction or promotion of mania Atropinic side effects Mild tremor Worsening of depressive symptoms Decreased appetite and weight loss Insomnia and hyperalertness Rash EKG evidence of cardiac conduction changes Hypertension
Sertraline	Children 25–100 mg qam Adolescents 50–200 mg qam	30–200	Depression OCD Migraine Depression with PDV	Same as fluoxetine except for excessive daytime sleepiness	Same as fluoxetine but infrequent hypovigilance Drowsiness Weight gain? Tremor Abnormal ejaculation/orgasm

Table 7. Antidepressant Pharmacotherapy (Continued)

Medication	Dosage Range	Serum Level (ng/mL)	Indications	Contraindications	Potential Adverse Effects
Trazodone	25–300 mg/d	800–1600	Depression Anxiety Insomnia	Obesity Excessive daytime sleepiness History of paroxysmal atrial tachycardia or other cardiac conduction disturbances Liver or renal disease (closely monitored) PDV	Induction or promotion of mania Atropinic side effects Mild tremor Worsening of depressive symptoms Increased appetite and excessive weight gain Excessive daytime sleepiness Rash EKG evidence of cardiac conduction changes Hypertension Priapism
Venlafaxine	25–200 mg/d	Not available	Depression Depression with PDV	Hypersensitivity to venlafaxine Hypertension History of paroxysmal atrial tachycardia or other cardiac conduction disturbances	Blood pressure change Nausea Drowsiness Dizziness Nervousness Abnormal ejaculation/orgasm

*Last dose should not be given after 4 PM.

EKG = electrocardiogram, OCD = obsessive-compulsive disorder, PDV = primary disorder of vigilance.

Adapted from Brumback RA, Weinberg WA. Pediatric behavioral neurology: An update on the neurologic aspects of depression, hyperactivity, and learning disabilities. Neurol Clin 1990;8:677–703; Levy HB, Harper CR, Weinberg WA. A practical approach to children failing in school. Pediatr Clin North Am 1992;39:895–928; and Weinberg WA, Schraufnagel CD, Chudnow RS, et al. Neuropsychopharmacology II: Antidepressants, mood stabilizers, neuroleptics (antipsychotics), and anxiolytics. In: Coffey EC, Brumback RA, eds. Textbook of Pediatric Neuropsychiatry. Washington, DC: American Psychiatric Press, 1998:1287–1350.

Table 8. Antimanic Pharmacotherapy (Mood Stabilizers, Neuroleptics, and Stimulants++)

Medication	Dosage Range	Serum Level	Indications	Contraindications	Potential Adverse Effects
++Adderall	Children 5–20 mg/d Adolescents 10–40 mg/d	Not available	"ADHD" PDV Hypomania	Hostile anger Depressive symptoms Hypertension Hyperthyroidism Glaucoma	Induction or promotion of depression Insomnia Tremor Headache Tic
Carbamazepine	Children 10–20 mg/kg/d Adolescents 200–1200 mg/d (use bid or tid dosage schedule)	4–12 µg/mL	Trigeminal neuralgia Partial, complex, and grand mal seizure disorders Diabetes insipidus Bipolar disorders Hostile anger/rages	Clozapine treatment History of bone marrow depression MAOI treatment within 21 days Hypovigilance Avoid erythromycin Petit mal seizures	Sedation/hypovigilance Ataxia Dizziness Diplopia Blurred vision Nausea Aplastic anemia/agranulocytosis Thrombocytopenia Elevated SGOT, SGPT, alkaline phosphatase Hyponatremia

Table 8. Antimanic Pharmacotherapy (Continued)

Medication	Dosage Range	Serum Level	Indications	Contraindications	Potential Adverse Effects
Clonidine	Children 0.05–0.1 mg bid or tid Adolescents 0.05–0.1 mg bid or tid	Not available	Bipolar disorders Tics "ADHD"	Cardiac abnormalities Hypotension Tachycardia Abnormal EKG change	Sleepiness Local redness and itching from skin patch Weight gain Temporary worsening of tics Headache Dizziness Abdominal pain Nausea or vomiting
Lithium carbonate	Children 20–40 mg/kg/d (600–1200 mg/d) Adolescents 600–1800 mg/d (use tid dosage schedule for regular tablets and bid schedule for sustained-release tablets)	0.8–1.4 mEq/L	Bipolar disorders Mental retardation with self-injurious behavior Prader-Willi syndrome Kleine-Levin syndrome Migraine Chronic tic disorder OCD	Pregnancy Significant renal or cardiovascular disease Dehydration Sodium depletion	Nausea Weight gain Excessive sedation Tremor Headache Neuropathy Acne Hypothyroidism EKG changes Polyuria Polydipsia

Table 8.   Antimanic Pharmacotherapy (Continued)

Medication	Dosage Range	Serum Level	Indications	Contraindications	Potential Adverse Effects
++Methyl-phenidate	10–60 mg/d (bid or tid dosages*)	Not available	"ADHD" PDV Hypomanic symptoms	Depressive symptoms Hypertension Chronic tic syndrome	Hypertension Induction or promotion of depressive symptomatology, particularly vegetative symptoms (anorexia, weight loss, insomnia, somatic complaints) Transient growth retardation Tics
++Modafinil	Children and adolescents 100–400 mg/d (qam or in 2 divided dosages)	Not available	Hypovigilance of narcolepsy PDV	Mania Unrecognized depression Hypertension Unstable angina	Possible induction of mania Headaches Elevated GGT enzyme
Olanzapine	Children and adolescents 2.5–10 mg/d in bid or tid dosage	Not available	Disorders of thought Hostile anger Agitation	Obesity Unrecognized depression	Obesity Sedation Depression Dyskinesia Tremor

Table 8. Antimanic Pharmacotherapy (Continued)

Medication	Dosage Range	Serum Level	Indications	Contraindications	Potential Adverse Effects
Quetiapine fumarate	Children and adolescents 25–200 mg in divided dosages (bid or tid)	Not available	Disorders of thought Hostile anger Agitation	Obesity Unrecognized depression	Obesity Sedation Depression Dyskinesia Tremor Hypotension Malignant hyperthermia
Risperidone	Children and adolescents 1–6 mg/d (preferably bid or tid)	Not available	Disorders of thought Hostile anger Agitation	Same as thioridazine	Obesity Sedation Depression Dyskinesias Tremor
Thioridazine	Children 10–15 mg bid, tid, or qid Adolescents 10–25 mg bid, tid, or qid	250–1250 (not used)	Psychotic features Aggression/hostile anger Mania Tic disorders Overanxious states Insomnia Paraphilias	Obesity Hepatic disease Excessive daytime sleepiness	Induction or promotion of depression Increased appetite and excess weight gain Excessive daytime sleepiness Rash Dyskinesias Retinitis EKG changes

Table 8. Antimanic Pharmacotherapy (Continued)

Medication	Dosage Range	Serum Level	Indications	Contraindications	Potential Adverse Effects
Valproate	Children 20–40 mg/kg/d (use bid or tid dosage schedule) Adolescents 375–1200 mg/d (dose as above)	50–100 μg/mL	Bipolar disorders Simple and complex absence seizures Generalized seizure disorders Migraine	Hepatic disease Pregnancy Pancreatitis	Nausea Sedation Tremor Weight gain Elevated SGOT, SGPT, alkaline phosphatase Hepatotoxicity Hyponatremia Pancreatitis Encephalopathy Thrombocytopenia Alopecia

*Last dose should not be given after 4 PM.

"ADHD" = attention-deficit hyperactivity disorder, PDV = primary disorder of vigilance, MAOI = monoamine oxidase inhibitor, SGOT = serum glutamic-oxaloacetic transaminase (aspartate aminotransferase [AST]), SGPT = serum glutamate pyruvate transaminase (alanine aminotransferase [ALT]), EKG = electrocardiogram, GGT = γ-glutamyltranspeptidase.

Adapted from Brumback RA, Weinberg WA. Pediatric behavioral neurology: An update on the neurologic aspects of depression, hyperactivity, and learning disabilities. Neurol Clin 1990:8:677–703; Levy HB, Harper CR, Weinberg WA. A practical approach to children failing in school. Pediatr Clin North Am 1992:39:895–928; and Weinberg WA, Schraufnagel CD, Chudnow RS, et al. Neuropsychopharmacology II: Antidepressants, mood stabilizers, neuroleptics (antipsychotics), and anxiolytics. In: Coffey EC, Brumback RA, eds. Textbook of Pediatric Neuropsychiatry. Washington, DC: American Psychiatric Press, 1998:1287–1350.

BIBLIOGRAPHY

Weinberg WA, Penick EC, Hammerman M, Jackoway M. An evaluation of a summer remedial reading program. A preliminary report on the development of reading. Am J Dis Child 1971;122:494–498.

Weinberg WA, Rutman J, Sullivan L, Penick EC, Dietz SG. Depression in children referred to an educational diagnostic center: diagnosis and treatment. J Pediatr 1973;83: 1065–1072.

Weinberg WA, Brumback RA. Mania in childhood: case studies and literature review. Am J Dis Child 1976;130:380–385.

Brumback RA, Weinberg WA. Mania in childhood. II. Therapeutic trial of lithium carbonate and further description of manic-depressive illness in children. Am J Dis Child 1977; 131:1122–1126.

Weinberg WA, Rehmet A. Childhood affective disorder and school problems. In: Cantwell DP, ed. Affective Disorders in Children and Adolescents—An Update. New York, Spectrum Publications, 1983:109–128.

Weinberg WA, McLean A. A diagnostic approach to developmental specific learning disorders. J Child Neurol 1986; 1:158–172.

Brumback RA, Weinberg WA. Pediatric behavioral neurology: an update on the neurologic aspects of depression, hyperactivity, and learning disabilities. Neurol Clin 1990;8: 677–703.

Weinberg WA, Brumback RA. Primary disorder of vigilance: a novel explanation of inattentiveness, daydreaming, boredom, restlessness, and sleepiness. J Pediatr 1990;116: 720–725.

Weinberg WA, Harper CR. Vigilance and its disorders. Neurol Clin 1993;11:1, 59–78.

Weinberg WA, Harper CR, Brumback RA. Use of the symbol language and communication battery in the physician's office for assessment of higher brain functions. J Child Neurol 1995;10(Suppl 1):S23–S31.

Weinberg WA, Harper CR, Brumback RA. Clinical evaluation of cognitive/behavioral function. In: Coffey CE, Brumback RA, eds. Textbook of Pediatric Neuropsychiatry. American Psychiatric Press, Inc. (APPI), Washington, DC, 1998: 171–220.

Emslie GJ, Weinberg WA, Kowatch RA. Mood disorders. In: Coffey CE, Brumback RA, eds. Textbook of Pediatric Neuropsychiatry. American Psychiatric Press, Inc. (APPI), Washington, DC, 1998:359–392.

Weinberg WA, Harper CR, Brumback RA. Attention-deficit/hyperactivity disorder III: disturbances of vigilance (wakefulness). In: Coffey CE, Brumback RA, eds. Textbook of Pediatric Neuropsychiatry. American Psychiatric Press, Inc. (APPI), Washington, DC, 1998:503–526.

Weinberg WA, Schraufnagel CD, Chudnow RS, Emslie GJ, Kowatch RA, Hughes CW, Brumback RA. Neuropsychopharmacology II: antidepressants, mood stabilizers, neuroleptics (antipsychotics), and anxiolytics. In: Coffey CE, Brumback RA, eds. Textbook of Pediatric Neuropsychiatry. American Psychiatric Press, Inc. (APPI), Washington, DC, 1998:1287–1350.

Brumback RA. Weinberg's syndrome: a disorder of attention and behavior problems needing further research. J Child Neurol 2000;15:478–480.

Schraufnagel CD, Brumback RA, Harper CR, Weinberg WA. Affective illness in children and adolescents: patterns of presentation in relation to pubertal maturation and family history. J Child Neurol 2001;16:553–561.

INDEX